JAMES GINDLESPERGER

Published by The History Press
Charleston, SC
www.historypress.com

Cover image: *Bayonet! Forward*, by Dale Gallon, www.gallon.com.

First published 2023

Manufactured in the United States

ISBN 9781467155229

Library of Congress Control Number: 2023938570

To the brave souls who earned the Medal of Honor, from a grateful nation.

I have said it time and again, and I will keep on saying it, that I would rather have a Medal of Honor than be President of the United States.

President Harry S Truman,
March 27, 1946

CONTENTS

ACKNOWLEDGEMENTS

When a reader picks up a nonfiction book, the only name that typically appears on the cover is that of the author. However, rarely is such a work the result of the author's sole effort. Books, by their very nature, only exist because of the input of a large number of people, even though it is the author who gets the credit. That is unfortunate because this book, like most such works, is the result of the much-appreciated assistance of many people behind the scenes. The contributions of those named here have been invaluable, and their assistance and encouragement are deeply appreciated.

I was writing a daily series of local historical articles on social media, including stories of some of our local military heroes. When I included a recipient of the Medal of Honor, I contacted the Congressional Medal of Honor Society for permission to use a photo of the man it had placed on its website. I soon received a reply from Laura Jowdy, archivist and historical collections manager for the organization, granting that permission. Laura also invited me to contribute a monthly account of some of the recipients of the Medal from the Civil War for the society's daily blog. Who wouldn't be honored to do something like that? I have been contributing something each month since September 2021, and in the process, I realized how much information we had to share. The society has provided much of the information about the men whose exploits I outline in this book, and I am indebted to Laura and the society for making that information available, as well as for furnishing most of the individuals' photos that appear in this work. She also graciously allowed me to adapt some of the articles I had already written for the society for inclusion in this book, which I deeply appreciated.

Other photos were provided by the Hall of Valor, the Department of Defense and the Library of Congress, and the Vigo County Historical Society provided a copy of the 14th Indiana Infantry's roster. Thanks to all of you.

Every book begins with an idea. Sometimes that idea foments in the mind of the author, but often it comes in the form of a suggestion from someone else. This book is the result of the latter. One of those who read my Congressional Medal of Honor Society blog contributions was Gerard Mayers, a friend from social media, who suggested I put them together into book form. My first reaction was that I had plenty to keep me busy without taking on another project, but the more I thought about it, the better it sounded. Gerard's suggestion became the basis for what you are about to read. Thank you, Gerard.

John Heiser, retired Gettysburg historian, has become a friend as well as an invaluable source of information. John had provided encouragement and information from the battlefield's archives for an earlier project that resulted in my award-winning book *Bullets and Bandages*. In the process of poring through the information that John had provided for that book, a great deal of incidental material also came to my attention. Much of that information was incorporated into this book, and I am indebted to John for that.

I would be remiss if I didn't acknowledge the help of my family. My wife, Suzanne; our daughter, Cheryl; and our son, Mike, have been supportive of all my projects from the very beginning, and I appreciate it. Suzanne, in particular, inadvertently helped ferret out much of the information that appears in this book, simply through all the effort she put into helping me research the field hospitals that were featured in *Bullets and Bandages*. Some of the information that didn't fit well with that book has been worked into *The Medal of Honor at Gettysburg*. In addition to my research partner, she is also a great travel companion, loyal confidante and best friend. I couldn't ask for a more supportive spouse.

I am also indebted to Dale and Anne Gallon for their permission to use Dale's painting *Bayonet! Forward* as the cover illustration. The use of this well-known painting will enhance the appearance of the book and make it an attractive addition to readers' bookshelves.

Thanks also to the Library of Congress, the Department of the Army and the various Licensed Battlefield Guides and park rangers for the information you have provided. I can't begin to thank all of you, not just for your help but also for the work you do.

To the many friends who expressed interest in this book, and for all their encouragement, thank you all very much.

The work to put this book together became a veritable labor of love, and I hope you enjoy the finished product. And by the way, never forget what our folks in uniform do and how we all benefit. Some have made the ultimate sacrifice; others have gone above and beyond the call of duty. All have earned our respect.

INTRODUCTION

It was the early summer of 1863. The Civil War had been going on now for two years, with no end in sight. Confederate General Robert E. Lee's Army of Northern Virginia had just gained a victory at Chancellorsville, and Lee decided to build on the victory by moving his army northward. His hope was that a bold offensive could derail Northern plans for the summer campaign and possibly demoralize the people of Maryland and Pennsylvania to the point where there may be enough pressure applied to President Abraham Lincoln that a peaceful agreement could be negotiated to allow the Southern states to leave the Union. Lee believed that his army could live off the land in the bountiful North and possibly even obtain badly needed supplies once there, giving the farmers of Virginia an opportunity to recover from the devastating effects of two years of war. A bonus would be a defensive movement by the Union that would take troops from the Siege at Vicksburg.

June 1 saw Lee's army moving swiftly toward Maryland. Federal troops followed a parallel path several miles east. A small skirmish between the Confederates and Union troops from New Jersey and Vermont took place on June 3, but otherwise Lee encountered little resistance.

For the next few days, Lee's army continued its northward march. Lieutenant General Richard Ewell took one arm through the Shenandoah Valley, General A.P. Hill took a second over a slightly different route through the Valley and Lieutenant-General James Longstreet took a third east of the Blue Ridge Mountains. Union General Joseph Hooker, believing that he was vastly outnumbered, planned to advance on Richmond but was countermanded by President Lincoln, who told him that the defeat of Lee's army was of more importance. Lincoln further ordered Hooker to stay between Lee and Washington. Hooker reluctantly followed Lincoln's orders.

On June 9, Major General J.E.B. Stuart encountered the Union cavalry under Major General Alfred Pleasonton at Brandy Station, Virginia. Confederate cavalry had proven superior to that of the Union throughout the first two years of the war, but in what is recognized as the largest cavalry battle to ever take place on American soil, Pleasonton's troopers proved up to the task. Although the daylong battle was considered a tactical victory for the Confederates, it marked the end of dominance by that army's cavalry.

FOUR DAYS AFTER THE Battle of Brandy Station, Ewell's Corps reached Winchester, Virginia, which was defended by a small force of some 7,000 men. With more than 12,000 troops, Ewell took Winchester in a three-day battle, inflicting nearly 4,500 casualties, with only 269 of his own. The fight was the second battle fought in Winchester, and it duplicated the Confederate victory of a year earlier.

Lee's advance continued for another week, with smaller skirmishes taking place along the way at Aldie, Middleburg and Upperville.

Meanwhile, on June 22, Confederate General Stuart had taken the bulk of the Confederate cavalry on a sweep behind the Union army, with orders to guard the mountain passes and screen Ewell's Corps. He was also expected to provide Lee with intelligence on the whereabouts of the Union army. Stuart, however, chose to raid Federal supply trains, and in doing so, he lost contact with Lee. Ultimately, by the end of June, Stuart's actions would prove fateful and take him out of touch with Lee for a week. He would not arrive at Gettysburg until the second day of the battle.

On June 27, Stuart was surprised at Fairfax Court House, Virginia, by a small patrol of men from the 11th New York Cavalry. Casualties were minimal, but the encounter further delayed Stuart's arrival at Gettysburg, compounding Lee's frustration.

On June 28, President Lincoln, tiring of General Joseph Hooker's reticence to fight, replaced him with General George Meade as the two armies approached Gettysburg.

By June 29, Ewell had reached the Cumberland Valley in Pennsylvania, not far from his objective of Harrisburg. Union Major General Darius

Couch had responded with troops of his own. Near Camp Hill, Couch had earthworks quickly thrown up as a defense. These fortifications became known as Fort Couch and Fort Washington. A small skirmish took place there the next day while, at the same time, Stuart engaged a cavalry force commanded by Brigadier General Judson Kilpatrick at Hanover.

Following the fight at Hanover, Stuart withdrew toward York, along with a captured wagon train. Having lost valuable time in the Hanover struggle, he was looking for either Ewell or General Jubal Early. Having to move more slowly than he would have normally, due to the logistics of protecting the captured wagon train, he reached the town of Dover early in the morning of July 1. As he rested his troopers, the Battle of Gettysburg was beginning.

While the early fighting was taking place at Gettysburg, Stuart was still unaware of Early's and Ewell's whereabouts. At Carlisle, he was delayed further by a skirmish in which he burned the Carlisle Barracks. The next day, he finally reached Lee's main army, too late to be of much use from an intelligence standpoint. He dispatched General Wade Hampton to a position at Hunterstown about four miles northeast of Gettysburg with orders to protect the left rear of the Confederate line. At Hunterstown, Hampton would engage two brigades from Judson Kilpatrick's cavalry division. One was commanded by Brigadier General Elon Farnsworth and the other by a brash, newly promoted brigadier general named George Armstrong Custer.

The main battle at Gettysburg was destined to last three days. Early on the morning of July 1, 1863, a Confederate division led by Major General Henry Heth approached the town of Gettysburg from the east. Although both armies had a good idea that the other was somewhere in the area, and with the sun barely above the horizon, Heth's men were surprised by a small cavalry force under Union Brigadier General John Buford. Although vastly outmanned, Buford's dismounted troopers held a better position and fought valiantly. With the advantage of breech-loading carbines as opposed to the Southerners muzzleloaders, they were able to hold off the larger Confederate force for several hours, long enough for the Union's Major General John Reynolds to arrive with his infantry from the First and Eleventh Corps. The cupola of the Lutheran Seminary became an observation and signal station for one side and then the other. In the early fighting, Confederate Brigadier General James J. Archer was captured by men from the Union's Iron Brigade.

Shortly after their arrival, Reynolds was killed, leaving the Federals without one of their most able commanders. Soon Confederate reinforcements under Generals A.P. Hill and Richard Ewell arrived, and the battle heated up, with thirty thousand Confederates opposing twenty thousand Federals. By late afternoon, the Union troops had been routed, falling back in a chaotic retreat through town, where they began to regroup on East Cemetery Hill. In the process, some four thousand Federal soldiers were taken captive among their ten thousand casualties.

FIGHTING TOOK PLACE INTO the night, with both sides saying later that they had to depend on the flashes from the muzzles of the guns to know where their enemy was. Hand-to-hand combat was common.

The primary areas where fighting took place that day were McPherson Ridge, Herbst Woods, the Railroad Cut, Oak Ridge, Seminary Ridge, in town, Culp's Hill and East Cemetery Hill. Aside from the death of Reynolds, a key element in the battle came when Lee ordered Ewell to "take that hill [East Cemetery Hill] if practicable." Ewell deemed it not to be feasible, choosing instead to await help from the Confederate Second Corps, which did not arrive until late in the day. Ewell's delay allowed the Union to gain command of the high ground, although Lee's use of the phrase "if practicable" has long been debated as too ambiguous for Ewell to be totally blamed.

The next morning, July 2, Lee began a series of attacks on Meade's flanks, which were now lined up in a battle line shaped like a fishhook, with the hook portion winding around Culp's Hill and the shank running toward Little Round Top at the south end. These attacks proved mostly unsuccessful, and both sides suffered heavy casualties.

That afternoon, Lee launched a heavy assault on the Union left flank. Commanded by Lieutenant General James Longstreet, ferocious fighting erupted at Devil's Den, Little Round Top, the Wheatfield, the Peach Orchard and Cemetery Ridge. Union Second Corps Major General Winfield Scott Hancock moved reinforcements quickly into position as a countermove. Lee's army launched full-scale assaults on East Cemetery Hill and Culp's Hill, gaining some ground but unable to dislodge Meade's men from their strong defensive positions. That night, Meade called several of his generals to his headquarters at the Widow Leister's farm on the back side of Cemetery Ridge. There he held a council of war, with the generals agreeing that, of all their options, the best course of action was to stand solid and fight again the next day.

Key elements of the day included Third Corps Major General Daniel Sickles moving his troops to a forward position in the Peach Orchard, leaving a gap in the Union line. The wisdom of this controversial move is debated to this day. In the ensuing fighting, his Third Corps was decimated and his leg was wounded so badly that it required amputation. Sickles would ultimately receive the Medal of Honor for his action, and his story appears later in this volume.

A second key element was the Confederate assault on Little Round Top, a hill at the south end of the fishhook that, if the Southerners could take it, would potentially allow the occupiers to destroy the Union line. Longstreet began his attack late in the afternoon. Neither side realized yet that Little Round Top was virtually undefended.

Fortuitously for the Union, Meade sent Brigadier General Gouverneur Warren to assess the area. Arriving on the scene, Warren saw that there were no defenders and sent dispatches to request troops be moved to the hill. A fierce battle soon was underway, a fight that ended with a famous bayonet charge by the 20th Maine Infantry driving the Alabama troops back. The 20th Maine produced two Medal of Honor recipients in this engagement, Sergeant Andrew Jackson Tozier and Colonel Joshua Chamberlain. Their stories are among those included later in this work.

As July 3 dawned, both Lee and Meade prepared for what would be the decisive third day of the epic battle. Meade's Council of War had made his decision simple: he would stand and fight, despite the heavy losses the Union army had suffered in the two previous days. For his part, Lee believed that he was winning the battle and planned to attack one final time to bring about a Southern victory. He would have Longstreet assault the Union's left, bolstered by fresh troops from Major General George Pickett's infantry division. Ewell would launch an attack with his Second Corps on Culp's Hill. To the east, Stuart's Cavalry would strike the Union from the rear while cutting off an avenue of retreat.

Unfortunately for the Confederates, Lee misread Meade's intentions, expecting him to maintain a defensive position while awaiting an attack. Instead, Meade, unknown to Lee, had ordered Major General Henry Slocum to drive the Confederates off Culp's Hill. A dawn attack showed Lee that Meade had no intention of passively waiting.

Longstreet's part in the Confederate assault was delayed by several hours, partly because Pickett's Division had not yet arrived as dawn broke and partly because Longstreet himself did not believe that a frontal attack would succeed. By the time Longstreet finally said he could be ready to attack by midmorning, Ewell was already fighting furiously on Culp's Hill, unable to provide assistance to Longstreet. Late in the morning, Ewell would break off the action on Culp's Hill after suffering heavy losses, dooming that portion of Lee's plan to failure.

Lee chose to attack the Union line with Pickett's Division, Major General Henry Heth's Division led by Brigadier General James Pettigrew and two brigades of Major General William Dorsey Pender's Division under the command of Major General Isaac Trimble. Two brigades of the Third Corps, commanded by Major General Richard Anderson, were assigned to provide support. Officially recorded as Longstreet's Assault or the Pickett-Pettigrew-Trimble Charge, the assault on the Union line on Cemetery Ridge became better known as Pickett's Charge.

The assault on the Union center began with a massive artillery barrage, the largest ever seen on the North American continent. Later reports claimed that the din could be heard in Pittsburgh, some 150 miles to the west. At the conclusion of the cannonade, the Rebel infantry stepped off on a mile-long march across open fields, receiving deadly fire as they got closer to the Federal line. One Confederate brigade, after intensive hand-to-hand combat, briefly breached the Northern line, but all were then captured, killed or driven back. Confederate Brigadier General Lewis Armistead was mortally wounded after leading his men through the line. The Union's First Lieutenant Alonzo Cushing was killed while directing the fire of the two remaining guns in what was originally a six-gun artillery battery. It would take 151 years, but Cushing would eventually be awarded the Medal of Honor for his actions that day. His story appears in Part V.

While Pickett's Charge was in progress, Stuart's Cavalry was engaged with Federal cavalry commanded by Brigadier General David M. Gregg at what would become known as East Cavalry Field. There was no decisive victor, although Gregg's action blunted Stuart's attack enough to deal a serious blow to Lee's plan to harass the Union line from the rear. Captain William Miller from the 3rd Pennsylvania Cavalry earned the Medal of Honor in this part of the fight, with a daring move that is also described in Part V.

Along the southern end of the battlefield, as Pickett's Charge was concluding, a lesser-known cavalry charge was taking place. In a senseless directive, Brigadier General Judson Kilpatrick ordered an assault by his cavalry against a well-fortified Confederate position marked by large boulders, stone walls and undulating terrain. The assault was easily repelled by the Southerners and resulted in the death of the Union's Brigadier General Elon Farnsworth. Major William Wells of the 1st Vermont Cavalry would earn the Medal of Honor in the action, with the account of his heroism also discussed in Part V.

Lee's army suffered casualties of nearly 60 percent, and the battle would be the high-water mark of the Confederacy. Never again would the Army of Northern Virginia reach so far into Northern territory. On July 4, 1863, Lee withdrew his troops from Gettysburg in a driving rainstorm. On his way southward, he came under harassment at several locations. Two Medals of Honor were earned along the way, one for actions at Monterey Pass and the other at the Battle of Williamsport. Those actions are described in detail in Part VI.

Part I

HISTORY OF THE MEDAL OF HONOR

The Medal of Honor is the highest award for valor that America can bestow on its military personnel. No other military award garners the admiration and respect that this award brings. Surprisingly, however, that was not always the case.

The Articles of War adopted by the U.S. Army in 1776 included a provision for recognition of those who distinguished themselves on the field of battle. That provision included only commissioned officers and established what became known as brevet promotions. Brevet promotions elevated the awardee a special higher rank. That rank was usually, but not always, the next higher rank and was preceded by the designation of "brevet." For example, a lieutenant colonel's bravery could be recognized by elevation to the rank of brevet colonel. The brevet rank accorded the bearer no additional pay or the right to a higher command; it was simply honorary, except in rare instances, such as a special assignment coming from the president of the United States. In those cases, the brevet promotion could include increases in pay and command responsibilities. Brevet promotions were utilized regularly until after the Civil War. Since the late nineteenth century, they have been utilized only sparingly. Commonly referred to as "frocking" today, their use is usually only temporary until an opening at the higher rank becomes available.

In 1782, George Washington created the Badge of Military Merit, the first such award to recognize individual heroism. After the Revolutionary War, however, there appeared to be no need any longer for a military award for valor, and the honor fell into disuse.

When the Mexican-American War broke out in 1846, however, the desire for a similar award arose, and in 1847, a Certificate of Merit was established for those who performed some form of gallantry in action. The certificate was upgraded to a medal, the Certificate of Merit Medal, in 1905.

Then, on December 9, 1861, a U.S. senator from Iowa, James W. Grimes, introduced legislation authorizing the awarding of medals to enlisted seamen and marines who showed "gallantry in action and other seamanlike qualities."

A similar proposal to Winfield Scott, the commanding general of the army, was rejected by General Scott, and thus the bill included no provision for any such award for those in the army. Just twelve days later, on December 21, 1861, President Abraham Lincoln signed the legislation.

The original Navy Medal of Honor was actually a pin that could be affixed to the uniform. The medal portion of the award was made by the Philadelphia Mint and consisted of a five-point star surrounded by a ring of thirty-four smaller stars, symbolizing the thirty-four states that formed the United States at the time. It is interesting to note that those thirty-four states included those that were attempting to secede, even though no Confederate soldier was eligible for the Medal. The center of the larger star contained the image of Minerva, the Roman goddess of war, dispatching the figure of Discord. The recipient's information was engraved on an open area. The Medal was suspended from a replica of a small anchor encircled by a rope, all of which were attached to a red, white and blue ribbon based on the flag. The attachments and presentation boxes were made by William Wilson and Sons, a Philadelphia firm.

On February 17, 1862, Senator Henry Wilson of Washington introduced a similar bill to create the Army Medal of Honor. Wilson's legislation specified that the award would be for noncommissioned officers and privates in the army who showed gallantry in action. The legislation became official on July 12, 1862, when President Lincoln affixed his signature. One year later, on March 3, 1863, army officers became eligible for the Medal, although naval officers would have to wait until 1915 to be included.

The Army Medal of Honor was similar to that of the navy's. An eagle holding a saber in its talons was depicted sitting on two crossed cannons, all of which replaced the Navy Medal's anchor. The bar holding the pin that attached the Medal to the uniform was also slightly different.

The first person to earn the Army Medal was Assistant Surgeon Bernard John Dowling Irwin of the 7th United States Infantry. His action took place on February 13, 1861, two months before the beginning of the Civil War.

On that date, Dr. Irwin voluntarily took command of a fourteen-man detachment and rescued Second Lieutenant George N. Bascom and sixty men who had been trapped by Chiricahua Apaches under the command of Chief Cochise. With the Medal of Honor still just a dream of Senator Grimes, Irwin's action got him the praise of his superiors but nothing else. It was not until 1894 that he was finally presented with the Medal.

The first Medal to actually be awarded was presented on March 25, 1863, by Secretary of War Edwin Stanton to six surviving members of a group of twenty-two Union soldiers who participated in a raid led by civilians James J. Andrews and William H. Campbell. In that raid, the group commandeered a locomotive at Big Shanty, Georgia, and headed north, destroying railroad tracks and bridges along the way. Private Jacob Parrott of the 33rd Ohio Volunteer Infantry was accorded the honor of receiving the first Medal by virtue of the punishment he had endured while a prisoner of war.

Less than two months later, the first Medal of Honor for action in the navy was awarded to Signal Quartermaster Robert Williams of the USS *Benton*. Receiving his Medal on May 15, 1863, for his actions during the Yazoo River Expedition, Williams was singled out especially for his heroism in a ninety-minute battle at Drumgould's Bluff in Mississippi. On July 10, 1863, Corporal John F. Mackie became the first member of the Marine Corps to receive the Medal. Mackie was recognized for maintaining a heavy musket fire against shoreline rifle pits when the USS *Galena* had attacked Fort Darling at Drewry's Bluff, Virginia, on May 15, 1862.

Shortly thereafter, the first controversy over the Medal arose. On April 16, 1864, a former slave named Robert Blake, then serving in the navy on the USS *Marblehead*, was awarded the Medal for his actions at the Battle of Legareville on the Stono River in South Carolina on Christmas Day 1863. Although there were undoubtedly those who believed that a Black man was not worthy of such an honor, that was not the real controversy. That arose some thirty-six years later when Sergeant William Carney of the 54th Massachusetts Infantry, the regiment featured in the movie *Glory*, was awarded the Medal of Honor for gallantry at the attack on Fort Wagner on July 18, 1863. Although he received his award on May 23, 1900, he was ultimately credited with being the first Black man to actually earn the Medal, since his action took place several months before Blake's, even though Blake was the first Black man to be presented with one. The honor of being the first Black man to be honored with a Medal of Honor thus depends on how the question is asked: was it when the Medal was earned or when the Medal was awarded?

The Navy Medal was revised in 1886, when the rope encircling the anchor was removed. The remainder of the medal was left untouched.

By 1896, veterans were beginning to hold reunions, and commemorative pins were given at these gatherings that looked much like the Medal of Honor. Member badges for various patriotic and political organizations had similar designs. The badge of the Grand Army of the Republic, or GAR, was virtually indistinguishable from the Medal of Honor. Those who had been awarded the Medal of Honor lobbied the U.S. Congress to grant exclusivity to the Medal of Honor design. Congress eventually acted on the request, and a committee headed by Medal of Honor recipient George L. Gillespie was given authority to redesign the Medal. That same year, the Army Medal's ribbon was revised, with the design based on the flag replaced by vertical red, white and blue stripes.

In 1897, the criteria for receiving the Medal of Honor were revised. No longer could a recipient nominate himself. Instead, nominations had to be corroborated by eyewitness statements, and the nomination had to come from someone other than the nominee. Further, the recommendation for the award had to be submitted within one year of the action that precipitated the nomination. A minor design change was also implemented, with the ribbon being modified. Congress also authorized a rosette that could be worn in lieu of the actual Medal.

Meanwhile, Gillespie's committee worked with Horace Porter, then the U.S. ambassador to France, to come up with a new design. Porter arranged for the French firm Arthur, Bertrand and Berenger to do the final design. The star shape was kept, but the goddess Minerva scene was modified to include only Minerva. The original oak leaf clusters on the points of the star were changed to a green enamel, and the outer edge was revised to include a wreath that surrounded the star. The crossed cannons on which the eagle sat were replaced by a bar inscribed with the word *Valor*, and the saber in the eagle's talons was replaced by an olive branch and a grouping of arrows. The reverse side of the medal contained space to inscribe the recipient's name and some details of his actions. The ribbon was replaced by the ribbon we see today, a blue background containing thirteen white stars.

The committee approved the French design, and on March 9, 1904, Gillespie submitted a patent application for the design before it could be copied. On November 22, 1904, Gillespie was issued U.S. Design Patent No. 37,326. One year later, he signed the patent rights over to Secretary of War William Howard Taft. The new design became known as the Gillespie Medal.

In keeping with the exclusive nature of the Medal of Honor, a more formal method of presentation was adopted. Since the very first Medal had been awarded, recipients often received their Medal through the mail, with no formal recognition. The luckier recipients received slightly more recognition by having their Medals presented at a simple military muster of their company or regiment. In 1905, that changed when President Theodore Roosevelt issued an executive order that established a formal presentation ceremony for future Medal presentations.

In 1913, the Navy Medal was revised again, with the red, white and blue ribbon being changed to the same shade of blue as that of the Army Medal. Six years later, the Navy Medal experienced another revision, this time to distinguish Medals awarded for actions in combat from those awarded for noncombat actions. That change incorporated a Maltese cross for heroic actions in combat rather than the star. Designed by Tiffany and Company, the Maltese cross version never caught on, and it was retired in 1942.

While the navy's version of the Medal had been in existence since 1861, officers of neither the navy nor the Marine Corps had ever been eligible for the award, no matter how heroic their actions had been. That changed on March 3, 1915, when the navy's eligibility rules were revised to allow those officers to also be eligible.

One year later, on April 27, 1916, Congress established the Army and Navy Medal of Honor Roll. It also passed legislation that provided a monthly pension for all Medal of Honor recipients when they reached age sixty-five.

Controversy arose once again in 1916 when an army review board examined every Army Medal that had been awarded up until that time. The reason for the review was to determine if those who had received the awards actually had met the standards for gallantry. The concerns about meeting the standards were well founded. Until that time, more than 2,600 Medals had been awarded. Of those, 864 had been presented to members of the 27th Maine Infantry during the Civil War as an inducement to get them to reenlist. Other obvious cases raising concern included Medals awarded to 4 officers and 25 enlisted men who had served as funeral guards when President Lincoln was assassinated. Another was awarded to a lieutenant colonel who had asked for one as a souvenir. Numerous other Medals had been awarded for less than gallant service, including that of William "Buffalo Bill" Cody and four other civilians who served as scouts during the Indian Wars. The review resulted in the rescinding of 911 Medals of Honor, although Buffalo Bill and his fellow scouts would have their honors restored in 1989 by a special act of Congress.

One of those rescinded was that of Dr. Mary Walker, who received hers for her devotion to the treatment of the wounded to the detriment of her own health, as well as the hardships she had suffered as a prisoner of war. Her Medal was rescinded because she was a civilian and had not mustered into military service. When the army's judge advocate general ruled that the army did not have the authority to require that the Medals be returned, however, Mary refused to return hers and wore it defiantly for the rest of her life. In 1977, after extensive lobbying by her descendants, her Medal was reinstated, making her the only woman to ever be awarded the Medal of Honor.

Early versions of both the Army and Navy Medals were usually pinned to the uniform breast, although it could also be pinned at the neck or worn attached to a ribbon around the neck. Shortly after the Navy Medal retired the Maltese cross version, the neck ribbon was officially adopted. The Army Medal did the same in 1944. Both changes also included an octagonal pad with thirteen stars on the ribbon, to which the Medal was attached. The changes were made to distinguish the Medal of Honor from all other military awards, an exclusivity that remains today.

In 1919, the Tiffany Cross was introduced as a new design for the Navy Medal. This new version was designated for those who earned their Medals for heroism in combat. The old version was kept for noncombat heroism. The Tiffany Cross was discontinued as of August 9, 1942, and the older design was retained as the exclusive Navy Medal.

In 1921, with World War I concluded, Congress sought a way to honor all the unknown dead who had fought in that war. A series of acts was passed authorizing Medals of Honor for representatives of all unknown casualties, including those of our European allies. The first such act, approved on March 4, 1921, authorized the president of the United States to bestow a Medal of Honor to an unknown British soldier buried at Westminster Abbey and another to an unknown French soldier buried at the Arc de Triomphe. In October 1921, a similar award was approved for an unknown Italian soldier interred in Italy's National Monument. With no unknown American soldier yet selected, it was ironic that America's highest military award went to three foreign unknown soldiers before one from the United States.

Following the actions of the European governments, Congress authorized the burial of one unknown soldier at Arlington National Cemetery, to represent all the unidentified remains of American participants in World War I. On November 11, 1921, that burial was conducted at the memorial, which has become known as the Tomb of the Unknown Soldier. President Warren G. Harding officiated and placed a Medal of Honor on the casket.

In December 1922, another act of Congress provided for the awarding of a Medal of Honor to an unknown Belgian soldier, followed by a similar act for an unknown Romanian soldier in May 1923. No awards of Medals for allied unknowns have been approved since then.

The custom of awarding a Medal of Honor to an American unknown soldier from subsequent wars has been followed for representatives from World War II, Korea and Vietnam. One unknown from each of those wars is also interred at the Tomb of the Unknown Soldier, and each has also been presented with the Medal of Honor. Ultimately, however, the remains of the unknown from Vietnam were identified as U.S. Air Force First Lieutenant Michael Blassie. The Medal originally awarded to him did not transfer with him when his remains were reinterred at Jefferson Barracks National Cemetery. The Medals awarded to American unknowns interred at the Tomb of the Unknown Soldier at Arlington National Cemetery, including the one originally awarded to Blassie, are displayed in a small museum under the Amphitheater at Arlington.

On May 24, 1943, the first and only award ever given to a member of the Coast Guard took place when President Franklin D. Roosevelt presented the Medal to the mother of Signalman First Class Douglas Munro for his heroism at the Battle of Guadalcanal. Munro was killed at the age of twenty-three in the performance of the action that earned him his Medal.

Guidelines for the awarding of the Medal were updated and approved by Congress on July 25, 1963. Those criteria are still in effect. The new guidelines provided for awards brought about by action while engaged against an enemy of the United States or while serving with friendly forces during armed conflict even if the United States is not a belligerent party.

Until 1965, members of the air force who were awarded the Medal of Honor received the army version. Then, a new version of the Medal was designed to provide the air force recipients with a version specific to their branch of service. The new Air Force Medal contained a figure of the Statue of Liberty rather than that of Minerva. The thirty-four stars were retained to symbolize the number of states in the Union when the Medal was first awarded. On January 1, 1967, Major Bernard Fisher received the first Air Force Medal for his rescue of a fellow airman who had crash landed in Vietnam.

In 1990, Congress passed Public Law 101-564 establishing March 25 of every year thereafter as National Medal of Honor Day, to officially honor those who have earned the Medal. The date was chosen to commemorate the date of the presentation of the first Medals of Honor on March 25, 1863.

Pension rules were relaxed on September 1, 2003, when the amount awarded to Medal of Honor recipients was increased to $1,000 per month. At the same time, the sixty-five-year-old age requirement was removed, and all recipients now receive this award.

Ten years later, on December 26, 2013, Congress extended the time limits for recommendation for the honor from one year after the action date to three years, and the Medal must now be presented within five years. An exception to that rule was made almost immediately. After a lengthy investigation by numerous interested parties, including several U.S. senators, the U.S. Army approved the nomination of First Lieutenant Alonzo Cushing of Battery A, 4th U.S. Light Artillery, for his actions on July 3, 1863, during Pickett's Charge at Gettysburg. There, despite several severe wounds, he directed fire against advancing Confederate forces until he was struck in the mouth by a bullet and fell dead across his gun. On November 6, 2014, the award was presented posthumously to First Lieutenant Alonzo Cushing. Cushing had left no direct descendants, so the Medal was presented by President Barack Obama to Helen Bird Loring Ensign, Cushing's second cousin twice removed.

As of this writing (March 1, 2023), 3,535 Medals have been awarded to 3,516 recipients. The numbers do not match up because there have been 19 double recipients. Their names, which follow, include their rank, service assignment and conflict or era for each award-earning action:

- Frank Baldwin, Captain, Company D, 19th Michigan Infantry—Civil War; First Lieutenant, 5th U.S. Infantry—Indian Campaigns

- Thomas Custer, Lieutenant, Company B, 6th Michigan Cavalry—Civil War (both awards)

- Henry Hogan, Private, Company G, 5th U.S. Infantry—Indian Campaigns; First Sergeant, Company G, 5th U.S. Infantry—Indian Campaigns

- William Wilson, Sergeant, Company I, 4th U.S. Cavalry—Indian Campaigns (both awards)

- Smedley D. Butler, Major, 3rd Battalion, 2nd Advanced Base Regiment, USMC—Mexican Campaign; Major, 2nd Marines, USS *Connecticut*—Haitian Campaign, 1915

- Daniel J. Daly, Private, Captain Newt Hall's Marine Detachment, 1st Regiment (Marines) USS *Newark*—China Relief Expedition (Boxer Rebellion); Gunnery Sergeant, 15th Company (Mounted), 2nd regiment, 1st Brigade, USMC—Haitian Campaign, 1915

- John Cooper, Coxswain, USS *Brooklyn*—Civil War; Quartermaster, Acting Rear Admiral Henry K. Thatcher's Staff, USS *Stockdale*—Interim 1865–70

- John King, Watertender, USS *Vicksburg*—Interim 1899–1910; Watertender, USS *Salem*, Interim 1899–1910

- John Lafferty (or Laverty), Fireman, USS *Wyalusing*—Civil War; 1st Class Fireman, USS *Alaska*, Interim 1871–99

- John McCloy, Coxswain, USS *Newark*, China Relief (Boxer Rebellion); Chief Boatswain, Pickett Launch, U.S. Navy, Mexican Campaign (Veracruz)

- Patrick Mullen, Boatswain's Mate, USS *Wyandank*—Civil War; Boatswain's Mate, USS *Don*—Interim 1865–70

- Robert A. Sweeney, Ordinary Seaman, USS *Kearsarge*—Civil War; Ordinary Seaman, USS *Yantic*—Interim 1871–99

- Albert Weisbogel, Captain of the Mizzen Top, USS *Benicia*—Interim 1871–99; Captain of the Mizzen Top, USS *Plymouth*—Interim 1871–99

- Louis Williams, Seaman, USS *Lackawanna*—Interim 1871–99; Captain of the Hold, USS *Lackawanna*, Interim 1871–99

- Louis Cukela, Sergeant, 66th Rifle Company, 5th Regiment, 2nd Division, USMC—World War I (both awards)

- Charles Hoffman, Gunnery Sergeant, 49th Company, 5th Regiment, 2nd Division, USMC—World War I (both awards)
- John J. Kelly, Private, 78th Company, 6th Regiment, 2nd Division, USMC—World War I (both awards)
- Matej Kocak, Sergeant, 66th Company, 5th Regiment, 2nd Division, USMC—World War I (both awards)
- John H. Pruitt, Corporal, 78th Company, 6th Regiment, 2nd Division, USMC—World War I (both awards)

There have been two father-son combinations to earn the Medal of Honor. In 1863, First Lieutenant and Adjutant of the 24th Wisconsin Infantry Arthur MacArthur Jr. earned his Medal for actions at Missionary Ridge, Tennessee. His son, General Douglas MacArthur, earned the Medal of Honor for his service in the defense of the Philippines in July 1941. The two were joined by Theodore Roosevelt for his actions at San Juan Hill in the Spanish-American War and his son Theodore Roosevelt Jr. for his during the Normandy Invasion of World War II.

Keeping with the familial theme, seven sets of brothers have also earned the Medal of Honor. Lieutenant Colonel John Black of the 37th Illinois Infantry earned his Medal in 1862 for actions at Prairie Grove, Arkansas, during the Civil War, while his brother William, captain in Company K of the same regiment as his brother, had already earned his for actions at Pea Ridge, Arkansas, nine months earlier. The brothers were presented with their medals in October 1893, just four weeks apart.

Charles and Henry Capehart both earned their medals for actions in the Civil War as well. Charles, whose story is featured elsewhere in this work, served as major of the 1st West Virginia Cavalry at Gettysburg, where he earned his Medal for actions on July 4, 1863, while pursuing Robert E. Lee's army. Colonel Henry, who eventually rose to general, served in the same regiment as his brother and earned his Medal on May 22, 1864, when he saved another man from drowning in the Greenbrier River while under fire.

A third pair of brothers also earned their Medals in the Civil War. With the war winding down, Private James G. Thompson and his brother, Private Allen Thompson, were serving in Company K of the 4th New York Heavy Artillery at White Oak Road, Virginia. On April 1, 1865, the brothers joined with five other men on a dangerous reconnaissance mission. Only two of the seven survived when they were attacked by Confederates. The two were James and Allen, although James was severely wounded. At the time of their action, Allen was seventeen years old and James was fifteen.

James and George Pond both earned their Meals in a lesser-known part of the Civil War, the fighting in Kansas. James, a first lieutenant in Company C of the 3rd Wisconsin Cavalry, earned his on October 6, 1863, at Baxter Springs, Kansas, when he and the two companies of cavalry under his command came under a surprise attack by a large number of guerrillas. Under his leadership, the cavalry was eventually able to drive the guerrillas out of the fortifications. James then went outside without any of his men, where he fired a howitzer three times to throw the guerrilla band into confusion and cause them to leave the area. Seven months later, George, as a private in the same company and regiment as his brother, earned his Medal. On May 15, 1864, he attacked a large band of guerrillas with only two other men at Drywood, Kansas. After routing the band, he and his two companions rescued several prisoners who had been held by the guerrillas.

On May 8, 1864, Private George Galloway of the 95th Pennsylvania Infantry's Company G earned the Medal at Alsop's Farm, Virginia, when he volunteered to hold a position that had come under heavy fire. He was successful and was awarded the Medal of Honor in 1895. While this action is admirable, it is interesting to note that George Galloway had been arrested the previous September for deserting his regiment the day before fighting began at Gettysburg. Obviously, he erased any doubts about his bravery at Alsop's Farm. His brother, Commissary Sergeant John Galloway, earned his own Medal as the war was winding down. On April 7, 1865, John, serving with the 8th Pennsylvania Cavalry at Farmville, Virginia, took it upon himself to ignore the danger and sprint through heavy gunfire to a point on the right of his regiment's line, which was in danger of collapsing. There, he rallied his men and prevented what was later referred to as an imminent disaster. He received his Medal two years after his brother.

Antoine and Julien Gaujot earned a place in history by earning their Medals in two separate wars, the only brothers to do so. Antoine was the first of the two to earn his. A corporal in Company M, 27th Infantry, U.S. Volunteers, he earned the honor at San Mateo, Luzon, in the Philippines on December 19, 1899. Captain Julien Gaujot of Troop K, 1st U.S. Cavalry, earned his Medal on April 13, 1911, at Aqua Prieta, Mexico, during the Mexican Campaign (Veracruz).

The last pair of brothers to earn the Medal were somewhat unique, in that they were Canadians serving on the same ship, the USS *Nashville*, and had volunteered for the same mission during the Spanish-American War. Seaman Harry Miller and his brother Willard, also a seaman, both earned their Medals on May 31, 1898, for their gallantry at Cienfuegos, Cuba.

The youngest recipient is William "Willie" Johnston, a drummer boy with Company D, 3rd Vermont Infantry. Willie was just thirteen years old when he was awarded his Medal for gallantry during the Seven Days Battles during the Civil War's Peninsula Campaign in June and July 1862.

Of the 3,535 medals awarded to date, 2,466 have gone to members of the U.S. Army, with 749 being credited to the U.S. Navy, 19 to the U.S. Air Force, 300 to the Marine Corps and 1 to the Coast Guard. Members of both the Marine Corps and Coast Guard receive the Navy Medals.

During the Civil War, 1,523 Medals of Honor were awarded, about 43 percent of all the Medals awarded to date. The Gettysburg Campaign accounted for 72 of those Medals. The pages that follow tell the amazing stories of these 72 men.

Part II

PRE-BATTLE, JUNE 1863

James Robinson Durham, Second Lieutenant, Company E, 12th West Virginia Infantry

The 12th West Virginia was relatively new, having been formed in August 1862. It hadn't seen any real action yet, with most of its early months spent in such mundane assignments as scouting and guard duty. Now it was June 1863, and the regiment was in Winchester, Virginia. The troops were getting restless. They wanted to see some action. Winchester had been the scene of a defeat for the Union army a year earlier, and if there was going to be another battle here, the Union army was determined that this time the results would be different.

Among those men was James R. Durham, serving as second lieutenant in the regiment's Company E. Durham was born on February 7, 1833, in the capital of the Confederacy, Richmond. He had moved from Richmond with his family at a young age, but he still often wondered what his old neighbors would think if they saw him marching down one of Richmond's streets with a Union regiment.

The Confederates had been on the march northward for nearly two weeks now, with the Union army marching not far from them in the same direction. A small skirmish had taken place ten days earlier, but the West Virginians had not been involved. Then word came back that the cavalry had been involved in a big battle at Brandy Station, but again, Durham and his comrades had only heard about it after the fact. While they weren't spoiling for a fight, the Mountaineers didn't sign up to spend their entire enlistment listening to others talk about their war experiences either.

James Robinson Durham. *Congressional Medal of Honor Society, Mount Pleasant, South Carolina.*

June 14, 1863, saw Durham and his men on a skirmish line, where they had been since the previous day, when it looked for a while like they might finally get to fight. However, it hadn't happened, and now the regiment was moving out in midafternoon without Durham. Company E had been selected to stay behind to provide cover. For the next two hours, Company E exchanged shots with some Georgia troops, but there still hadn't been any real fighting.

Late in the afternoon, Durham watched from behind a stone wall as the rest of the regiment returned, along with the 122nd and 123rd Ohio Infantries. When all had formed up behind the wall where Durham and Company E were positioned, the order came. Company E was now to advance toward what looked like the entire Confederate army, now positioned a short distance ahead in a well-protected defensive location. Durham opined that the situation could not be more dire.

Still, he knew that he had to obey his orders, and he gave the order to his men to rise up from behind the wall and move forward. As soon as they did, they were met with a barrage from their foes. Durham was wounded almost immediately, but he pressed on at the front of his line. Leading his men despite his wounds, Durham and Company E routed the Georgians, who retreated to the safety of a more distant stone wall.

With their mission completed, Durham ordered his men to fall back to their starting point. Only then did Durham take the time to examine his wounds. Finding his right hand and arm shattered, he walked to the regiment's hospital in Winchester for treatment. He would lose several fingers, along with the use of his hand, as a result of his wounds.

Despite the Union army's desire for a better outcome at the Second Battle of Winchester, it was not to be. Lee's army ultimately routed the Union troops and continued its advance toward Gettysburg. Confederate casualties were estimated at about 300, while the Federals lost some 4,400, including nearly 4,000 prisoners.

After Durham recovered from his wounds, it was determined that he was no longer fit for combat, and he was relegated to serving on several courts-martial, as well as on the commission in command of the ambulance corps for the First Infantry Division of the Department of West Virginia.

On March 6, 1890, Lieutenant James R. Durham was presented with the Medal of Honor. In a significant example of understatement, his citation reads simply:

> *Led his command over the stone wall, where he was wounded.*

On August 6, 1904, Durham passed away. He was buried in Section 3 of Arlington National Cemetery.

JOHN THOMAS PATTERSON, PRINCIPAL MUSICIAN, 122ND OHIO INFANTRY

ELBRIDGE ROBINSON, PRIVATE, COMPANY C, 122ND OHIO INFANTRY

It would be fair to think that someone who served as a musician would never be in a position to earn the Medal of Honor. After all, the primary role of the musicians was simply to entertain the troops and provide music while the army was on a march. They also played appropriate music for funerals and provided rallying music during battles. None of this sounds very dangerous. However, as with many things, that is an oversimplification. Those may have been the duties under normal circumstances, but two musicians in the 122nd Ohio Infantry were not your normal musicians and what they were about to encounter was not a normal circumstance.

John Patterson was born in rural Morgan County, Ohio, on February 3, 1838, to James Polk Patterson and Mary Whiteside Patterson. He was one of only two boys in a family of eight children. On January 1, 1862, less than a year after the Civil War broke out, he married Lizzie E. Bell. Eight months later, the newlywed answered a call for troops, traveling to Zanesville, Ohio, and joining Company C of the 122nd Ohio Infantry. He enlisted on August 22, 1862, and was officially mustered in on October 2 that same year with the rank of musician. He was promoted to principal musician just six days later.

Elbridge Robinson was also born in Morgan County, Ohio, and he and Patterson had been friends back home, although Robinson, born on January 7, 1844, was younger. While not much is known about Robinson's early years, it is known that he married Marietta Reichart and that they had a daughter. His enlistment and muster dates are identical to Patterson's, so it is likely that the two friends traveled to Zanesville together to enlist.

Elbridge Robinson. *Congressional Medal of Honor Society, Mount Pleasant, South Carolina.*

Because the musicians practiced together and had something in common, they tended to stick together when they were not performing their duties. In doing so, Patterson and Robinson developed a close friendship with one of the regimental drummers, Price Worthing. The three were said to be inseparable.

At the Second Battle of Winchester, the 122nd Ohio was ordered to move forward on June 14, 1863, with its sister regiment, the 123rd Ohio, to engage the Confederates in an area known as Bower's Hill. It was during this action that James Durham's 12th West Virginia Infantry had been left behind to provide covering fire. The story of Durham's action to merit the Medal of Honor was discussed earlier. Patterson and Robinson were destined to earn Medals of their own that same day.

The musicians hung back slightly as the Ohioans skirmished on Bower's Hill. Fighting became intense, and eventually the order was given to fall back. Patterson and Robinson, along with the other musicians, scurried back to the stone wall they had left not long before. Those already safely behind the wall calmed themselves with nervous laughter at how ridiculous some of their comrades looked as they labored to crawl over the wall.

Patterson reflexively looked around to see if anyone of his friends was missing. At first it appeared to him that everyone had returned safely. Then he realized that Worthing was not there. As principal musician, Patterson felt a responsibility for the other musicians. Not seeing Worthing, Patterson's concern grew, and he inquired of the other musicians if they had seen him. None had.

Patterson feared that Worthing may have been left behind when the regiment fell back. At about the same time, he heard Robinson also asking about Worthing. The two looked at each other and then nodded without saying a word. Both knew that they were about to go looking for their friend.

Patterson told Sergeant Ellis Miller his plan, pointing to Robinson as he said it. Then, peering over the stone wall, the two noticed that the Confederates appeared to have fallen back as well. The battlefield was strangely silent. Nothing moved. Nervously easing themselves over the wall, Patterson and Robinson crouched to make themselves smaller targets, but their movements attracted the attention of Confederate skirmishers, who began shooting at them.

Concealing themselves behind whatever cover presented itself and moving only when the Rebels paused to reload, the two slowly worked their way back toward Bower's Hill, where the regiment had recently been fighting. The pattern of secreting themselves behind trees and boulders as each volley resounded, and then moving stealthily forward as their adversaries reloaded, continued for several minutes.

Then, in a lull in the shooting and with the woods eerily silent, they heard a slow, rhythmic tapping as they moved toward Romney Road. Reaching a small hedgerow, they spotted someone in a Union uniform lying a short distance away. Before even reaching the injured soldier, they knew it was their eighteen-year-old friend, Worthing, who was tapping with a broken stick on the stock of a discarded weapon, hoping to attract attention. He had been shot through both legs and could not move.

Reaching him, Robinson feared that the youth would not survive. His eyes were closed, and he was pale from the loss of blood, more pale than Robinson had ever seen a man. Patterson leaned over the motionless Worthing and whispered that he and Robinson were going to get him back to safety. Worthing's eyes flickered, the first indication to his rescuers that he was still alive.

Patterson and Robinson gently raised Worthing and began the laborious task of half carrying, half dragging the helpless youth, who moaned in pain with every bump. Sporadic shots came their way, some coming so close that the balls passed through their clothes, but none did any damage.

Then, with the woods beginning to look familiar, indicating that the three were nearing their destination, another barrage rang out. This time a Rebel bullet struck the luckless Worthing in the leg. Worthing cried out in pain just moments before all three were knocked to the ground by the force of an exploding Union artillery shell. None of them spoke for several seconds, each trying to catch his breath. Finally, the protracted effort to return Worthing to the safety of the Union line resumed.

As the wall came into sight through the underbrush, the Rebel guns resumed their torrent of fire, this time striking Patterson. Injured badly, Patterson urged Robinson to assist Worthing the remaining few yards as the pursuing Rebels drew closer. Robinson and Worthing reached the wall just as the Confederates reached Patterson. With the men of the 122nd Ohio

Patterson grave marker. *Author photo.*

firing at them, the Southerners grabbed Patterson and carried him off. He would spend much of the rest of the war as a prisoner at Belle Isle and Libby Prison, both in Richmond. He was eventually released and was able to rejoin the 122nd Ohio in time for the final battle at Appomattox Court House. He was present at Lee's surrender.

Unfortunately, however, the heroic rescue effort had been for naught, as Worthing eventually died from his wounds.

Patterson and Robinson both mustered out on June 26, 1865, and Patterson returned to Ohio. He and Lizzie and their children later moved to Wisconsin, where he bought a farm. Robinson also returned to Ohio for a time and then moved to Vernon, Illinois, where he became active in civic affairs in the town of 350 inhabitants. The town of Vernon became home to several Civil War veterans, and on May 30, 1915, the town dedicated its Veterans Park on one acre of land donated by Robinson. Each veteran, or a relative of a deceased veteran, planted a tree.

On April 5, 1898, Robinson received the Medal of Honor for his heroic effort. One year later, on May 13, 1899, Patterson was presented with the Medal for his actions at Winchester. Both citations were identical:

> *With one companion, voluntarily went in front of the Union lines, under a heavy fire from the enemy, and carried back a helpless, wounded comrade, thus saving him from death or capture.*

Lizzie Patterson passed away in 1902, and Patterson remarried in 1906 to Sarah Harris. The Civil War hero lived until March 3, 1922. He was buried at Oakwood Cemetery in Mauston, Wisconsin. He had outlived Robinson, who died on January 19, 1918, by four years. Elbridge Robinson's remains were buried at Patoka Cemetery in Patoka, Illinois.

Nathan Mullock Hallock, Private, Company K, 124th New York Infantry

Nathan Mullock Hallock was born on August 23, 1844, to James Blizzard Hallock and Melinda (Mullock) Hallock. Nathan's mother died just a few days after he was born, and young Hallock was raised by his grandmother and two aunts.

Just days before his eighteenth birthday, he enlisted in the 124th New York Infantry, the famed Orange Blossoms, and was assigned to Company K.

On June 15, 1863, the 124th New York was on the march with the rest of the Union army's Third Corps as it followed Robert E. Lee's army in their trek northward. The 124th had just reached Bristoe Station, Virginia, when Lieutenant Lewis Wisner could go no farther in the intense heat. Suffering from what appeared to be sunstroke, he collapsed. Despite the temperature, the regiment had to stay on the march with the rest of the corps, and Captain William A. Joseph directed Hallock to remain behind with Wisner to assist him.

When guards from the 15th Vermont left, Hallock and Wisner were alone. Their solitude didn't last long, however, as Confederate scouts soon entered the deserted Union camp. Seeing the two blue-clad New Yorkers, the Rebels began shooting. Ignoring Wisner's orders to leave him and find safety for himself, Hallock helped the weakened Wisner to his feet and half carried, half dragged him to a location where they couldn't be seen by their assailants.

Several hours later, an ambulance arrived to remove Wisner to an aid station. As the ambulance approached, however, the Confederates once again opened fire, forcing the ambulance driver to retreat several hundred yards. Hallock knew that their only chance to avoid capture or, even worse, lay with that ambulance. Once again, he wrestled Wisner to his feet and slipped his arm around his companion's waist. Pulling Wisner's arm over his own shoulder, Hallock somehow avoided the heavy gunfire sent in their direction and dragged him to the ambulance. Once at the aid station, Wisner quickly recovered and rejoined the regiment in time to be with them at the Battle of Gettysburg.

In a touch of irony, Wisner was with Hallock on July 2 when Hallock fell while the regiment fought at Devil's Den—not from a bullet, but from sunstroke.

Hallock survived his bout with the heat, as well as the war, and returned to his home in Middletown, New York, and began to work in a bank. He received a number of promotions until the bank closed. Not long later,

The unlucky Hallock suffered sunstroke and, later, a broken ankle while visiting the same area around the regiment's monument. *Author photo.*

Hallock obtained employment as chief cashier at the Merchants National Bank in Middletown, where he eventually rose to the office of president.

In 1884, Hallock returned to Gettysburg for the dedication of the monument to the 124th New York. Halleck's luck at Gettysburg was no better the second time. While walking in the same general area where he suffered his sunstroke more than twenty years earlier, Hallock tripped on the uneven ground and broke his ankle.

On September 10, 1897, Hallock was awarded the Medal of Honor for his actions at Bristoe Station. Hallock's citation read:

> *At imminent peril saved from death or capture a disabled officer of his company by carrying him under a hot musketry fire to a place of safety.*

His award resulted from his nomination from none other than Wisner, who had earned the award himself for his actions at Spotsylvania.

In 1903, Hallock was hiking with two friends at the Grand Canyon when he took ill. When he eventually regained his strength and felt he could travel, the three made their way to Los Angeles, where his condition deteriorated. Diagnosed with pneumonia, he passed away at age fifty-nine on March 21, 1903. His remains were returned to Middletown, New York, where he was buried at Hillside Cemetery.

LUIGI PALMA DI CESNOLA, COLONEL AND BREVET BRIGADIER GENERAL, 4TH NEW YORK CAVALRY

The Second Battle of Winchester was still fresh in the minds of the troops of both sides when, just two days later, the cavalries met at the village of Aldie in Loudon County, Virginia. The Confederates were taking advantage of the terrain, using the Blue Ridge Mountains to hide their position. J.E.B. Stuart's Cavalry was serving as an effective screen that hindered the Union effort to pinpoint where Lee's army was and where it was headed.

On June 17, 1863, newly minted Brigadier General Judson Kilpatrick's Brigade chanced upon Virginia troopers under Confederate Colonel Thomas Munford. While not a huge battle (about 2,000 Union soldiers went up against some 1,500 Confederates) when compared with battles such as Gettysburg, Chancellorsville, Shiloh and others, the four-hour fight had no outright victor but served to delay the Union cavalry, which was seeking out the Army of Northern Virginia.

One of those present for the fight at Aldie was Colonel Luigi Palma di Cesnola of the 4th New York Cavalry. Di Cesnola, a native of Italy, was born on June 29, 1832, in Rivarola, Piedmont, Italy, the son of a count and military officer. He had a strong military background, having joined the Sardinian army at age fifteen and been decorated for bravery and promoted in the First Italian War for Independence at the age of sixteen. In 1851, he graduated from the Royal Military Academy and eventually served as aide-de-camp to General Enrico Fardella in the Crimean War.

Luigi Palma di Cesnola. *Congressional Medal of Honor Society, Mount Pleasant, South Carolina.*

Di Cesnola moved to New York in 1858, marrying Mary Isabel Reid, the daughter of Commodore Samuel Chester Reid, a veteran of the War of 1812 who assisted in designing the 1818 version of the United States flag. The young Italian founded a private military school, so when the Civil War began, he was well versed in military protocols. Feeling some allegiance to his new country, he joined the 11th New York Cavalry as a major.

Within months, his military career took a decided downturn when he was arrested and imprisoned for plotting a mutiny among his men, although he was soon released and transferred to the 4th New York Cavalry as a lieutenant colonel, ascending to the rank of colonel when the regiment's Colonel Christian Dickel resigned his commission.

His troubles were not to end with his release, however. Within months, he was accused of stealing six pistols from the government when a box, addressed to Di Cesnola's wife and containing the pistols, was seized by the provost marshal. Despite Di Cesnola's protest that the pistols were to be given to the regimental recruiting officer as a tool for preventing recruits from deserting, he was dishonorably discharged on February 3, 1863.

Deciding to fight for his honor, Di Cesnola contacted Secretary of War Edwin Stanton, showing that the recruiting officer had indeed signed a receipt for the weapons. One month after his discharge, he was reinstated to command of the 4th New York Cavalry.

When the Battle of Aldie began, Di Cesnola was under arrest. Accounts for the reason behind his arrest differ. One claimed that his arrest was for vocally protesting the promotion of another officer to brigadier general. Another account claimed that he had been arrested because some of the men under his command had ridden through the ranks of an infantry regiment, implying that he did not control his troops. The real reason may never be known for certain.

One thing that is without dispute, however, is that his saber and sidearm were taken from him at the time of his arrest. Without Di Cesnola as its leader, the 4th New York Cavalry hesitated several times when it was expected to charge a gun battery. Seeing the men's reluctance, General Judson Kilpatrick released Di Cesnola from arrest and gave him his own sword, supposedly telling Di Cesnola to "bring it back to me covered in the enemy's blood."

Di Cesnola rushed to the front of his troopers, rallied them and then led them in two charges. The New Yorkers were successful in overrunning the battery on the second try, taking one hundred prisoners in the process. Di Cesnola, however, was wounded, suffering a saber wound to the head and a bullet wound to his arm. When his horse was shot from under him, he was captured and taken to Libby Prison in Richmond, where he remained until 1864, when he was exchanged for a personal friend of Confederate President Jefferson Davis. He mustered out of service on September 4, 1864.

In March 1865, he was recommended for a brevet promotion to brigadier general, but the war ended before the U.S. Senate could act on the recommendation.

Di Cesnola's postwar career was a series of achievements. He was appointed U.S. consul to Cypress and discovered thousands of antiquities while there. However, Cypress considered Di Cesnola to be guilty of looting, despite a special committee finding him to be innocent. The items in question were later purchased by the Metropolitan Museum of Art in New York, and in 1879, he became the museum's first director. He became an author and received honorary degrees from both Princeton and Columbia Universities, as well as special knightly orders from both Bavaria and Italy.

On December 6, 1897, he was awarded the Medal of Honor for his actions at Aldie. His citation read:

> *Was present, in arrest, when, seeing his regiment fall back, he rallied his men, accompanied them, without arms, in a second charge, and in recognition of his gallantry was released from arrest. He continued in the action at the head of his regiment until he was desperately wounded and taken prisoner.*

Di Cesnola died on November 20, 1904, and was buried at Kensico Cemetery in Valhalla, New York, three days later. Accounts of his funeral service at St. Patrick's Cathedral in Manhattan indicate that more than two thousand mourners, including hundreds of dignitaries, were in attendance.

Thomas M. Burke, Private, Company A, 5th New York Cavalry

On June 30, 1863, the citizens of the town of Hanover were uneasy. Just east of Gettysburg, they had endured a Confederate raid by cavalry led by Lieutenant Colonel Elijah White three days earlier. Now, amid rumors of more fighting to come, Union cavalry under Brigadier General Elon Farnsworth and Brigadier General George Armstrong Custer were in town. The Union troops had arrived early that morning, and the people of the town had provided them with food.

Throughout the morning, minor skirmishes took place along the route followed by Major General J.E.B. Stuart toward Hanover. Several regiments of Union troops had just passed through town when Stuart's Confederate cavalry slammed into the rear guard. Panic-stricken citizens ran for cover anywhere they could find it as the fighting erupted all around them. In the confusion, an ambulance guard from the 5th New York Cavalry was run over by one of his own ambulances, and he suffered mortal injuries.

Reinforcements arrived for both sides. The advantage swayed first to one side and then the other. Despite the seriousness of the situation, one incident that brought laughs from several Union soldiers occurred when Confederate Lieutenant Colonel William Payne was tossed into a tanning vat by his dying horse. He was fished out and taken captive by a group of highly amused Federals.

The battle moved through town to the Forney farm, where the Federals took a stand. In the confusion, Stuart found himself nearly surrounded. He saved himself, along with a staff officer, by racing his horse through heavy fire, at one point leaping his horse across a wide ditch.

Thomas M. Burke. *Congressional Medal of Honor Society, Mount Pleasant, South Carolina.*

The fighting culminated with a two-hour artillery duel, with several buildings in the town hit by shells. The encounter delayed Stuart once again in his effort to locate Ewell, depriving Lee of knowing just where the Union army may be. The struggle resulted in 215 casualties on the Union side and 117 on the Confederate. There was no conclusive victor.

Private Thomas M. Burke, as part of Company A of the 5th New York Cavalry, was in the thick of the fight. Born in Ireland in 1842, he had mustered in with the New Yorkers in October 1861. With the Confederates in a hotly contested control of the town, Burke and the rest of the 5th New York Cavalry had regrouped under the direction of Major John Hammond. Just a few blocks from the town square, the New Yorkers launched a charge, scattering surprised Confederates. The goal of Hammond's men was to capture a battery that was inflicting major damage on the Federals.

When they got closer to the battery, Burke and Corporal James Rickey each spied a Confederate flag in the possession of two mounted members of the 13th Virginia. Both rushed toward it. As they closed the distance, Rickey's horse was shot, leaving Burke alone in the race to the flag. Reaching the two Virginians in charge of the flag, Burke raised his gun and ordered the men to surrender.

The Confederates had not seen Burke through the smoke until it was too late for them to react. Almost immediately they surrendered. Burke ordered them to throw down their weapons and then escorted the two, along with their flag, to the Union line, where Burke turned them over to General Kilpatrick.

After being discharged, Burke reenlisted. In February 1864, he was part of a small detachment that made its way across Confederate lines to destroy railroads, bridges and telegraph lines. Disguised as Confederate soldiers, the group encountered other Confederate soldiers, who quizzed them concerning their destination. Apparently, Burke and his companions provided satisfactory answers, and they no doubt breathed a sigh of relief when their challengers allowed them to go on their way, sparing them from likely execution as spies.

On February 11, 1878, Burke was presented with the Medal of Honor for his action at Hanover. His citation could not be simpler:

> *Capture of battle flag.*

In receiving the Medal, Burke became the first recipient to earn the Medal in a Civil War battle on free soil.

Later, Burke submitted a request for a second Medal for his actions behind Confederate lines in 1864. Although it was permissible at that time for a soldier to nominate himself for the Medal of Honor, his request was rejected by the War Department on the basis of his having already received a Medal.

Burke died on March 15, 1902, and was buried at Calvary Cemetery in Woodside, New York.

Part III

THE FIRST DAY OF BATTLE, JULY 1, 1863

Jefferson Coates, Sergeant, Company H, 7th Wisconsin Infantry

Jefferson Coates, also known as Francis Jefferson Coates, was born in Boscobel, Grant County, Wisconsin, on August 24, 1843, the eldest of six children born to William and Cynthia (Cain) Coates. Anxious to join the Union army when the Civil War broke out, he enlisted just five days after turning eighteen, joining on August 29, 1861. He mustered in on September 2, 1861, as a corporal in Company H of the 7th Wisconsin Infantry, which became part of the famed Iron Brigade.

Coates saw his first action at Second Bull Run, nearly a year after mustering in. That battle resulted in a Union defeat, and Coates lost several of his friends in the battle. The Maryland Campaign followed, with several more companions becoming casualties. Coates was wounded at the Battle of South Mountain on September 14, 1862, one of the Union's 2,325 casualties. The wound was more painful than serious, and Coates was proud of the part he played in the Union victory.

Less than a week after the fight at South Mountain, the 7th Wisconsin fought at Antietam before a short period of inactivity. Coates welcomed the break in the action, using the time to fully heal from his South Mountain injury. He was injured a second time at Fredericksburg on December 13, 1862, where he received a severe stomach wound. Then came the march to Gettysburg, where his life changed forever.

Jefferson Coates. *Congressional Medal of Honor Society, Mount Pleasant, South Carolina.*

On July 1, 1863, Coates, the 7th Wisconsin and the rest of the Iron Brigade clashed with part of Brigadier General James J. Archer's Brigade on McPherson Ridge. Fighting was brutal, and Archer was captured, the first Confederate general officer taken captive since Robert E. Lee had taken command of the Army of Northern Virginia.

The 7th Wisconsin fought valiantly, and none fought harder than Coates. Fighting at close quarters became hand-to-hand combat. Bayoneted in his side, Coates refused to stop fighting. His courage was inspirational for his comrades, and he was credited with sparking the effort that pushed Archer's men off McPherson Ridge. At the peak of the fighting, however, he was shot in the face. Unable to see, he could only listen helplessly to the din of the battle.

When his friends were forced to retreat, Coates lay helplessly until a compassionate Confederate officer, perhaps having seen the courage with which Coates had fought, guided the nineteen-year-old to the safety of a nearby tree. There, the man gave Coates some water, while Coates, in turn, offered his benefactor some of his coffee.

Coates was found four days later, still leaning against the tree, his sight permanently gone. Moved first to the Lutheran Seminary field hospital and then to the Satterlee Hospital in Philadelphia, he was discharged for disability on September 1, 1864.

Following his discharge, Coates chose to move on with his life as best he could. He learned to read braille. Needing a means of supporting himself, he took up the trade of broom making. On June 29, 1866, his heroics at Gettysburg earned him the Medal of Honor. His citation recognizes the ferocity with which he fought:

> *Unsurpassed courage in battle, where he had both eyes shot out.*

On April 21, 1867, less than a year after receiving the Medal of Honor, he married Rachel Drew and moved to Dorchester, Nebraska, where he and Rachel reared five children. Refusing to let his disability limit him, he farmed, became active in local community affairs and served on the local school board.

Coates fell ill with pneumonia at age thirty-six and passed away on January 27, 1880. He was first laid to rest near his beloved farm but was reinterred in 1888 at the Dorchester City Cemetery.

Note: This section was adapted from one that originally appeared on the website of the Congressional Medal of Honor Society.

EDWARD LYONS GILLIGAN, FIRST SERGEANT, COMPANY E, 88TH PENNSYLVANIA INFANTRY

It was early afternoon on July 1, 1863, when the 88th Pennsylvania Infantry formed a line along the Mummasburg Road. The 88th Pennsylvania Infantry had not yet fought on this day, although the regiment, along with Company E's twenty-year-old First Sergeant Edward Gilligan knew it was only a matter of time. The Pennsylvanians had been in this position before, with the butterflies in the stomach, the prayers, the thoughts of home and the disposing of playing cards and any other items a man didn't want to have found in his pockets if he ended up being killed. These men were battle tested—having already fought at such places as Cedar Mountain, Second Bull Run, South Mountain, Antietam, Fredericksburg and Chancellorsville—and now it appeared that they would be engaged at Gettysburg at any moment.

Born on April 18, 1843, in Philadelphia, Gilligan and several of his boyhood friends mustered into the 88th Pennsylvania as privates on October 22, 1861, and Gilligan took quickly to the life of a soldier. He had been promoted to sergeant in a very short time and was well liked and respected by the rest of the men in his company. He rose to first lieutenant and ultimately to captain in 1864.

As Gilligan reflexively jerked with the roar of a nearby cannon, his friend Captain Joseph H. Richards shouted to him to get his men prepared to charge. Brigadier General Henry Baxter's Brigade had just routed a brigade of North Carolinians under Confederate Brigadier General Alfred Iverson on Oak Ridge, and the 88th Pennsylvania was ordered to launch an assault on the retreating enemy.

Gilligan led his men in the charge, the acrid smoke burning his eyes. The field was littered with so many bodies that it was difficult to maintain any order. Leaping over the prone figures, he and his men caught up with the slower men of the 23rd North Carolina. Just to his left he spied Captain

Richards engaged in a struggle with the North Carolina color bearer. It looked like Richards was in trouble.

Gilligan abruptly changed direction and rushed to the aid of his captain. The color bearer, in keeping with the honor of guarding the colors with his life, pulled the flagstaff from Richards's hands and turned his attention to the onrushing Gilligan. Before the man could get into a position to provide much resistance, Gilligan struck him with the butt of his musket, knocking the man to the ground. Gilligan quickly grabbed the colors before the man could regain control and ordered the color bearer to surrender. All around him, Gilligan could see most of the North Carolinians also giving up the fight. When the action settled, the 88th Pennsylvania had taken dozens of prisoners from the hard-hit men of Iverson's Brigade.

Edward Lyons Gilligan. *Congressional Medal of Honor Society, Mount Pleasant, South Carolina.*

Gilligan had the opportunity to show his mettle once again, as well as his quick thinking, at a raid to destroy the Weldon Railroad in December 1864. By this time, Gilligan had been promoted to captain and acting adjutant of his regiment and was therefore on horseback. Confederate cavalry scattered many of his men, and he rode back to rally them. Unsuccessful, Gilligan found himself alone and facing the Rebels as they retreated following a Union countercharge. Realizing that he would not be able to get away, he slid out of his saddle and threw himself onto the ground.

With the Union army hard on their heels, the Confederates did not have the luxury of stopping to capture one lone Federal. The Southerners rode their horses directly over Gilligan as he lay in the muddy road, slashing at him with their sabers as they passed. Gilligan scrambled desperately to avoid both the saber attacks and the pounding hooves as the Rebel cavalry passed.

Showered with mud but miraculously uninjured, he rose and remounted when he was satisfied that the last horseman had passed. His return to his regiment was greeted with surprised shouts from his men, who had assumed that he had either been captured or killed.

Gilligan survived the war despite suffering wounds at Hatcher's Run and Boydton Plank Road in the closing days of the war. He mustered out and returned to the Philadelphia area, where in March 1872 he married

Frederica Beeroth. Tragically, his bride contracted peritonitis and died at age twenty-three just six months later.

Employed by the Philadelphia, Wilmington and Baltimore Railroad, Gilligan met and married Cora Estella Orr in 1876, who waved to him each time his train passed through her town. The couple moved to the village of Oxford, Pennsylvania, where Gilligan became the chief engineer on the train to Baltimore. He became involved in various civic activities in Oxford, including founding the first Boy Scout troop in the town.

On April 30, 1892, he was awarded the Medal of Honor for his actions at Gettysburg. His citation read:

> *Assisted in the capture of a Confederate flag by knocking down the color sergeant.*

Edward Gilligan breathed his last on April 2, 1922, and was interred at the Oxford Cemetery.

Henry Shippen Huidekoper, Lieutenant Colonel, 150th Pennsylvania Infantry

Beyond the extraordinary bravery exhibited by Medal of Honor recipients without exception, we often fail to realize the pain many of them endured while performing the actions that earned them their Medal. Some seem almost superhuman. Such a man was Lieutenant Colonel Henry Shippen Huidekoper of the 150th Pennsylvania Infantry.

Huidekoper was born in Meadville, Pennsylvania, on July 17, 1839, the eldest son of Edgar and Frances (Shippen) Huidekoper. As a young boy, he had seen his grandfather assist several escaped slaves in their journey to freedom. That experience shaped his own ardent opinions against slavery. Shortly after his graduation from Harvard College, he and his brother Frederic enlisted into the 150th Pennsylvania Infantry. Commissioned as a captain, he became the regiment's lieutenant colonel one month later.

Late in the morning of July 1, 1863, Huidekoper and his 150th Pennsylvania Infantry arrived at Gettysburg from its camp in Emmitsburg. Almost immediately they were ordered to throw off every piece of equipment except their guns, haversacks and canteens and move to a point along what today is Stone-Meredith Avenue near the McPherson farm. Protected only by a small fence, they awaited an assault. When it came, they fired a volley along with the 143rd and 149th Pennsylvania Infantries, driving the assault back. Taking advantage of the Rebels' confusion, the Federals mounted a charge that some sources say resulted in the recapture of the colors belonging to the 149th. Other sources indicate that the regiment's colors had never been taken in the first instance. Whichever is true, the colors were safely in the hands of the regiment at this point. Later, however, the colors were lost and the color guard taken captive when the Union line broke.

Henry Shippen Huidekoper. *Congressional Medal of Honor Society, Mount Pleasant, South Carolina.*

Following the charge, the 150th fell back to its original position, coming under intense fire from an advancing Confederate line. Losses were heavy, and the Union troops were forced to fall back even farther. When Colonel Roy Stone was wounded, Colonel Langhorne Wister assumed command of the brigade and Huidekoper took Wister's place in command of the regiment. Wister's stint as brigade commander was short-lived however. He was shot in the mouth, a wound bad enough that he was forced to relinquish command.

Huidekoper's fate wasn't much better. First wounded in his right leg, he then suffered a severe wound to his right arm. Other officers urged him to get to an aid station quickly before he lost so much blood that he might not survive. Huidekoper, however, had other ideas. He may have had the use of only one arm, but he could still command. He even believed that he could still fire a weapon with his good arm if he needed to. A second wound to the same arm still failed to deter him. He stayed in command for several more hours until there was a lull in the fighting. Only then did he agree to seek medical attention. Reluctantly, he gave up command of the regiment to Captain Cornelius Widdis. Widdis was taken captive not long after.

In extreme pain, Huidekoper wrapped a tourniquet above his shattered elbow to stem the flow of blood and then undertook a walk of more than a mile to a field hospital at the St. Xavier Catholic Church on West High Street in town. There, surgeons determined that his arm could not be saved. Two days after it was amputated, Huidekoper moved to the home of Peter Myers just down the street from the church, where he remained until he was placed on the wet floor of a freight car that had been used to haul ice to

Gettysburg. After a twelve-hour trip, he arrived in Baltimore, where he was taken to a general hospital. He returned to Gettysburg several times after the war to visit the Myers family.

Two months later, he returned to his regiment. However, the severity of his wound proved to be too much, and he resigned from the army in 1864 and returned to his hometown of Meadville, Pennsylvania. He married Emma Gertrude Evans a few months later. They would eventually have two children.

In 1870, he accepted an appointment as major general in the Pennsylvania National Guard. President Rutherford B. Hayes appointed him postmaster of Philadelphia in 1880, a position he held until 1885. In addition to serving in several high-level positions in both business and military organizations, he became an overseer at Harvard in 1890, serving for twelve years.

On May 27, 1905, he was awarded the Medal of Honor for his actions at Gettysburg, his citation reading:

> *While engaged in repelling an attack of the enemy, received a severe wound of the right arm, but instead of retiring remained at the front in command of the regiment.*

Huidekoper was afflicted with an unknown illness in the fall of 1918 that required him to be admitted to Polyclinic Hospital in Philadelphia. He succumbed to that illness on November 9 and was returned to Meadville for burial at the town's Greendale Cemetery.

Francis Irsch, Captain, Company D, 45th New York Infantry

Born on December 4, 1840, in Saarburg, Germany, Captain Francis Irsch was one of more than 200,000 German Americans to serve in the Union army. On July 1, 1863, he found himself in Gettysburg with his regiment of other German Americans, the 45th New York Infantry, under the command of Colonel George Van Amsberg. Irsch was commanding four companies of the 45th on the first day of fighting at Gettysburg.

Irsch and his four companies had just moved forward with orders to take Moses McClean's barn on Oak Hill when they came under heavy artillery fire. Their advance halted, Irsch ordered his men to seek cover until reinforcements arrived. When Dilger's and Wheeler's Batteries arrived with the rest of the 45th New York, the advance resumed until troops from Alabama were encountered. Dilger's Battery immediately responded, firing several volleys into the midst of

Francis Irsch. *Library of Congress.*

the Alabamians and sending them into disarray. Seeing their confusion, Irsch decided to strike while the opportunity was there. He ordered his men to charge, the action driving the Rebels into the teeth of fire from the 12th and 13th Massachusetts Infantries. As Confederate casualties mounted, parts of three Southern regiments surrendered, while several of their comrades took cover in McClean's barn. Irsch and his men then stormed the barn, adding more than one hundred prisoners to the total already captured.

Unfortunately for Irsch and the rest of the Union's Eleventh Corps, the tide soon turned. Within hours, the corps was routed, as was the First Corps. A chaotic retreat into town took place, with the Confederates in hot pursuit. Once in town, the detritus of war blocked streets, making further efforts to reach the rest of the Union army on East Cemetery Hill futile. What little semblance of order quickly disappeared, with the 45th New York breaking up into small groups and frantically attempting to reach a place of safety.

Irsch and several of his men reached Chambersburg Street, where they made a defensive stand that has often been compared to the stand taken by Texas defenders at the Alamo. Irsch is reported as having instructed his men, "Stand here and die or perish in captivity. Imprisonment or death!"

Irsch was with a group in the Eagle Hotel. Others occupied nearby homes. As a group they fought for nearly two hours. By late afternoon, however, the Union troops were surrounded, with little hope of breaking through the Confederate line. A Southern officer demanded their surrender. After consultation among those with him in the hotel, Irsch stepped out onto the street under a flag of truce to speak with the Rebels. An enemy officer showed him what he was up against, and Irsch was convinced that any further fighting would accomplish nothing and that he and his men had no chance of escape. He returned to his men with the news, and after much discussion, it was agreed that after destroying their weapons and ammunition, they would surrender. His actions are credited with delaying the Confederate advance through the town, thus providing time for more Union troops to reach the safety of East Cemetery Hill.

Irsch and his officers were taken to Libby Prison in Richmond, where he would take part in the famous tunnel escape in February 1864. He was recaptured and returned to Libby, and over the next several months, he was moved through prisons in Macon, Georgia; Danville, Virginia; and finally Charleston, South Carolina. He was eventually paroled on March 1, 1865.

On May 27, 1892, Irsch was awarded the Medal of Honor for his actions on July 1, 1863. According to his citation, he exhibited:

> *Gallantry in flanking the enemy and capturing a number of prisoners and in holding a part of the town against heavy odds while the Army was rallying on Cemetery Hill.*

Irsch died on August 19, 1906, and was buried at Woodlawn Cemetery in Tampa, Florida.

JAMES MONROE REISINGER, CORPORAL, COMPANY H, 150TH PENNSYLVANIA INFANTRY

The 150th Pennsylvania Infantry had the rare honor of having two of its members earn the Medal of Honor in the same action. The first of these, Lieutenant Colonel Henry Huidekoper, is discussed earlier. The second, Corporal James Monroe Reisinger, earned his shortly after Huidekoper's wounding.

Reisinger was born in Beaver County, Pennsylvania, on October 28, 1842, to Charles and Providence (Roberts) Reisinger, the sixth of seven children in the family. After attending college for a year, he dropped out and began working in the Pennsylvania oil fields. On August 28, 1862, he enlisted in the 150th Pennsylvania Infantry.

On July 1, 1863, he was serving as a color corporal for the regiment on McPherson Ridge in Gettysburg. He had fought in the early assault described in the account of Huidekoper's action and was engaged once again around midafternoon near Edward McPherson's barn. Although McPherson, a former congressman, was the owner of the farm, it was leased to John Slentz and his family at the time of the battle.

At about 2:00 p.m., Reisinger received his first of three wounds when he was struck in the right foot. The bullet shattered the bones of the instep and lodged in the ball of his foot. The pain from this wound was so severe that Reisinger later noted that he could not put weight on his foot for at least ten

James Reisinger was wounded three times in the vicinity of the 150th Pennsylvania Infantry monument. His heroism earned him the Medal of Honor by a special act of Congress in 1907. *U.S. government photo.*

minutes. Color Sergeant Samuel Peiffer urged Reisinger to go to the rear, but after discovering that he could stand on his heel, he refused to go as long as the regiment was engaged.

Using a fence for cover, the regiment fought and then made a charge. Running into heavy resistance, the men fell back to the fence and made a stand until they were set upon from the left flank. When orders were given to fall back, the regiment made a fighting retreat until it reached the McPherson house. There, it made another stand. The troops made another charge and then another retreat, illustrating the ebb and flow of the fighting in that area.

As they passed the McPherson house a second time, Reisinger was wounded again, this time when a ball struck him just behind the right knee and lodged against the bone. The impact knocked Reisinger to the ground. Someone, believed to be Corporal Samuel Barnes, assisted Reisinger to his feet. At this point, Sergeant Peiffer was carrying the colors with one hand, his other arm rendered useless by a ball that had passed through the bicep. Most of the color guard had similarly been incapacitated. When Reisinger was ordered to the rear to receive medical assistance, he again refused, arguing that the fighting was so intense that the regiment needed every available man.

By now, Reisinger was hobbling badly and having some difficulty keeping up with the regiment. As the regiment moved toward the Lutheran Seminary, he sustained yet another wound. This time the ball struck him in the lower portion of his right hip, passing through the lower part of the hip and lodging in the fleshy portion of his thigh. Falling to the ground once again, he found himself now so weak that he could scarcely raise his gun.

When the fighting abated, he was taken to the St. Xavier Catholic Church in town. On July 10, the ball in his hip was removed by an army surgeon. The other two remained in his body for a year, with the one in his knee removed in May 1864 while he was home on leave. The third was removed two months later by a surgeon named Brown at the Augur General Hospital in Alexandria, Virginia.

Reisinger recovered from his wounds but walked with a decided limp for the rest of his life. He served in the Veterans Reserve Corps, as well as with the 114th U.S. Colored Troops as a first lieutenant.

In 1904, Reisinger applied for the Medal of Honor, but his request was denied by the War Department. Enlisting the aid of his friend Senator Boies Penrose, a special act of Congress awarded him the Medal on January 19, 1907, with the actual presentation coming on January 25, 1907. His citation didn't do his heroism justice, saying in a classic understatement:

> *Specially brave and meritorious conduct in the face of the enemy. Awarded under Act of Congress January 25, 1907.*

Reisinger lived until May 25, 1925, when he died of complications from influenza. He was buried in Meadville, Pennsylvania, at the Greendale Cemetery.

James May Rutter, Sergeant, Company C, 143rd Pennsylvania Infantry

Sergeant James Rutter had been fighting since 11:00 a.m. the morning of July 1, 1863. It was now 4:00 p.m., and he, along with his comrades in Company C of the 143rd Pennsylvania Infantry, were tired. Tired in the fatigue sense and also just plain tired of being shot at. The regiment had only been formed five months earlier, and they were already tired of war, truth be told. They had taken a beating at Chancellorsville in their first real fight, and here they were at Gettysburg and things weren't going any better.

Rutter was born in Wilkes-Barre, Pennsylvania, on May 13, 1841, where his regiment had been formed. Now, the twenty-two-year-old hoped to see his twenty-third birthday. The 143rd had just had a narrow escape, having been nearly completely surrounded, and a rapid retreat had been ordered.

As Rutter struggled to catch his breath and calm his nerves, Lieutenant John Kropp shouted that it would not be right to leave their wounded Captain George Reichard behind as they retreated. He asked for volunteers to bring the captain off the field. Although the captain was well liked, nobody was of a mind to expose himself to the heavy fire that was still pouring into their ranks. Kropp asked again. Rutter jumped to his feet immediately, despite the fire from the Rebels on the opposite side of a small railroad cut that momentarily separated the two opponents.

Rutter heard himself saying that he would do it, although he wasn't thrilled about the idea. The captain lay along the Chambersburg Pike in front of the firing line. Looking at the wounded man, then at the Confederate troops just a short distance away, he thought that they couldn't miss him if they shot at him from that distance.

He scrambled to the captain's side and lay down beside him to make himself as small a target as possible. Rutter asked the captain if he could walk. Getting an affirmative answer, he assisted Reichard to a crouching position, hoping that the smoke of battle would conceal them. Maintaining a low profile, Rutter put his arm around Reichard's waist while the latter placed his own arm across Rutter's shoulder, and the two began a half run, half walk in the direction of the Union line. Reichard's wound prevented them from moving quickly, and their shadowy forms caught the attention of the Rebels in spite of the poor visibility. The balls whizzed past their heads but failed to find their mark.

James May Rutter. *Congressional Medal of Honor Society, Mount Pleasant, South Carolina.*

Reaching a fence that slowed their travel even more, another member of the regiment who had seen the two struggling to cross the fence line used his gun and knocked the top two rails off to allow them to cross. Rutter could see the men of the 143rd firing as they retreated, and it was only a few minutes later that Rutter and Reichard found themselves caught in a crossfire as they neared the Lutheran Seminary.

Throwing themselves to the ground to avoid being shot, possibly by their own men, Rutter was surprised to see a friend, Private George Tucker, walking upright toward them and giving no indication that he was aware he was being shot at. Rutter pulled him to the ground beside Reichard and, seeing blood running down Tucker's face, asked him where he had been hit. Tucker didn't answer, instead standing back up and walking in the direction of the Confederate firing line.

Rutter called to him and yelled at him to come back, that he was going toward the wrong side. Tucker wordlessly turned around and, childlike, walked back. It was obvious to Rutter that his friend had suffered some form of brain injury; placing Tucker on one side and Reichard on his other, he laboriously got them to the safety of the Union line.

Once back with his company, Lieutenant Kropp delegated Corporal George Kindra to help Rutter carry Reichard into town because there were no stretchers or ambulances available. Tucker followed behind, and the four safely reached town, where they left Captain Reichard at a private home that was already filling up with wounded. As they did that, Tucker wandered off. Rutter would not see him again until several days later, after he had been treated and returned to the company.

Leaving the house that had become a makeshift field hospital, several men from Company C ran past them, frantically warning them that the Southerners were right behind them. Kindra and Rutter began their own running retreat through an alley and several open fields until they reached the safety of an old cemetery, where they took refuge. When the fighting finally tailed off, Rutter and Kindra rejoined the regiment, which had reassembled nearby.

On March 14, 1865, Rutter transferred to the Signal Corps and returned home to Wilkes-Barre. While he would never forget that day in Gettysburg, the ordeal slowly worked its way into the recesses of his memory. Then, on October 30, 1896, he learned that he was to receive the Medal of Honor for his heroism. His citation read:

> *At great risk of his life went to the assistance of a wounded comrade, and while under fire removed him to a place of safety.*

James Rutter passed away on November 23, 1907, at the age of sixty-six. He was buried at Hollenback Cemetery in his hometown.

ALFRED JACOB SELLERS, MAJOR, 90TH PENNSYLVANIA INFANTRY

Born in Bucks County, Pennsylvania, on March 2, 1836, Alfred Sellers enlisted in the 19th Pennsylvania Infantry, a three-month regiment. When the 19th Pennsylvania was reorganized as the 90th Pennsylvania, Sellers became the regiment's major. He was wounded in his right leg at Fredericksburg in December 1852.

On the afternoon of July 1, 1863, Sellers and the 90th Pennsylvania were on Oak Ridge in Gettysburg, where the ebb and flow of battle was illustrated perfectly. The Union troops had pushed their Confederate counterparts back earlier in the day. However, the Southerners were not about to give up, reorganizing and launching an assault of their own on the Federal left flank at Willoughby Run.

The 90th Pennsylvania, along with the remainder of the First Corps, had regrouped along Seminary Ridge. While this placed the First Corps into a better defensive position, it had the effect of leaving the Eleventh Corps' left flank exposed. When the Confederates initiated a follow-up attack, the Union line was breached near the center, plunging the line into disorder. The Eleventh Corps was overwhelmed and soon gave way. The breakdown took a part of the First Corps with it, and the Federal troops dissolved into disarray. The Rebel army was now in control of the town.

When the Eleventh Corps line crumpled, the 90th Pennsylvania was on Oak Ridge. An immediate action was needed or the First Corps right flank would be turned. Major Alfred Sellers, one of the oldest men in the regiment at age twenty-seven, saw the danger and jumped into action. Although he was not in command, he rushed to the front and took charge. He had been badly injured at Fredericksburg, suffering a broken leg, and he could have been forgiven if he had been reluctant to jump into danger

Alfred Jacob Sellers. *Congressional Medal of Honor Society, Mount Pleasant, South Carolina.*

after nearly losing his life once under similar circumstances. However, Sellers was not one to give in to fear, and his show of confidence in the face of heavy fire inspired the men of the regiment to follow. When he ordered a change of front, the men immediately acted, while three regiments from Colonel Edward O'Neal's Brigade—the 6th, 12th and 26th Alabama—bore down on him.

With the assistance of Captain Hubert Dilger's Battery, the position change allowed the 90th Pennsylvania to meet the Alabamans' charge and turn them away, inflicting heavy losses and saving the First Corps flank, as well as the entire Eleventh Corps.

Sellers was discharged from service on February 29, 1864. Returning to his home in Plumsteadville, Pennsylvania, he resumed a life of relative normalcy, but he wasn't forgotten. On March 13, 1865, he received a brevet promotion to lieutenant colonel and colonel in a show of respect for his gallantry. On July 21, 1894, his actions at Gettysburg garnered him an even greater recognition, the Medal of Honor, with his citation reading:

> *Voluntarily led the regiment under a withering fire to a position from which the enemy was repulsed.*

Alfred Sellers died on September 20, 1908, in Philadelphia after a series of strokes. He was buried at Mount Vernon Cemetery in that city.

FRANCIS ASHBURY WALLER, CORPORAL, COMPANY L, 6TH WISCONSIN INFANTRY

Francis Waller (spelled "Francis Asbury Wallar" in some sources), who preferred to be called Frank, was such a committed soldier that his former company commander would say at Waller's funeral that Frank never missed a roll call in the four years he served. That dedication was even more remarkable when his regimental affiliation is considered. The 6th Wisconsin was a part of the Iron Brigade, known for its participation in many of the Civil War's bloodiest battles. The sight of their trademark Hardee black hats was often enough to strike fear into the hearts of the bravest men in the Army of Northern Virginia, and their willingness to fight made their members who made it unscathed through the entire war extremely rare. The brigade suffered a 61 percent casualty rate at Gettysburg. Frank Waller was one of those who made it through.

Waller was born on August 15, 1840, to David and Marian Waller. When Frank was in his early teens, the family moved from Sunday Creek, Ohio, to western Wisconsin. In the summer of 1861, Frank and his two brothers, Samuel and Thomas, joined the Anderson Guards, which would become Company L of the 6th Wisconsin Infantry.

His dedication and bravery were never more on display than on the first day of fighting at Gettysburg, July 1, 1863. The regiment had helped push back the first Confederate offensive that morning in Herbst Woods. The retreating Southerners took refuge in a nearby railroad cut, where they returned what was described as a murderous fire. When the 6th Wisconsin scaled a fence in preparation for mounting a charge, the men were joined by the 95th New York Infantry and the 14th Brooklyn Infantry.

The three regiments moved forward in a steady advance, firing as they moved. Waller, spying the flag of the 2nd Mississippi Infantry, angled his march toward the flag bearer. Observing several blue-clad bodies at the feet of the color bearer already, Waller knew that his task would not be an easy one. Reaching the man, he leveled his weapon on him and demanded that he relinquish the colors. The color bearer, however, was prepared to defend his prize and resisted initially. Then, just as Waller lunged for the flag, the color bearer was shot. Waller grabbed the staff before the colors touched the ground.

Only feet away, a Confederate raised his gun in Waller's direction. Just as he squeezed the trigger, a Union soldier struck the Rebel's gun upward, deflecting the shot and saving Waller's life. That Union soldier was Waller's own brother, Samuel.

Waller would say later that his immediate thought was to take the flag to the rear straight away so it could not be retaken. However, with fighting still occurring, he threw the flag to the ground, stood on it to maintain control and loaded and fired twice.

When a man from the 14th Brooklyn attempted to take the flag from Waller, the latter threatened to shoot him if he persisted. Finally, Lieutenant Colonel Rufus Dawes ordered Major J.A. Blair to surrender his 2nd Mississippi troops. Seeing that further fighting was futile, Blair offered Dawes his sword.

Waller captured the 2nd Mississippi Infantry's flag near the monument on the left, the 6th Wisconsin monument. *Author photo.*

With the fighting now suspended, Waller and several others were ordered out on a skirmish line. Before complying, he asked Colonel Dawes what he should do with the flag. Dawes said that he would take it to the rear for him. Spying a wounded Sergeant William Evans of Company H going that way for treatment, Dawes handed him the flag, with orders to take it back with him. Before reaching an aid station, however, Evans was captured. He was held for two days before returning to the regiment when Lee's army retreated. While Evans was a captive, several ladies from Gettysburg helped him to successfully hide the captured colors, which he was able to bring to the regiment upon his return.

Over the next eighteen months, Waller was showered with praise for his action and was promoted from corporal to sergeant to first sergeant to second lieutenant. The greatest recognition, however, came on December 1, 1864, when he received the Medal of Honor. His citation read:

> *Capture of flag of 2d Mississippi Infantry (C.S.A).*

At war's end, Waller became a farmer in Wisconsin, married Mary Hall in 1868 and had six children. He also found time to serve as the Vernon County sheriff in 1880.

Unfortunately, as often happens, there were others who wished to usurp the glory that Waller had earned. Two other members of the 6th Wisconsin, independent of each other, claimed that they had been the ones to actually capture the flag. First, Frank Hare, formerly of Company B, claimed in 1880 that he had been the one to capture it. A friend alerted Waller that Hare had made the assertion, and Waller responded with the same commitment he had exhibited as a soldier. He immediately obtained sworn affidavits from others who had been there that day, along with official documents. Seeing this information, Hare then insisted that he had captured someone's flag that day. If it wasn't the 2nd Mississippi's, it must have been some other Confederate banner. He was then presented with evidence that the regiment had captured only the 2nd Mississippi's flag at Gettysburg, prompting him to meekly withdraw his claim.

Three years later, perhaps unaware that the matter of who captured the flag had already been settled, Cornelius Okey, who had been a private in the regiment's Company C, published an article telling in great detail how he had captured the flag, suffering serious wounds in doing so. He claimed to have given the flag to a sergeant from Company H within minutes, presumably Sergeant Evans, before he went to the rear for medical attention. He said that the sergeant, whose name he could not recall, had visited him while he was recuperating from his wound and provided him with a statement claiming that he (the sergeant) had also been wounded and had handed the flag to Waller before going for his own medical treatment.

By this time, Waller was living in Petonka, South Dakota. A copy of Okey's article was sent to him, with a request that he comment on Okey's claim. The fiery Waller responded with the same zeal he had exhibited on the battlefield. In a letter to the *Milwaukee Sunday Telegraph*, he opened his comments by calling Okey a liar, expressing his doubts that Okey was even at Gettysburg (he was). Waller then went on with a detailed account of how the flag had been taken. He closed by referring to Hare's claim, offering to provide Okey copies of the affidavits of those who had confirmed that it had been Waller who had captured the flag.

In Okey's defense, several of the members of the 6th Wisconsin had been killed or wounded in an effort to capture the flag before Waller's success. Okey had been one of those wounded and had actually been able to grasp the staff before being wounded, a fact that Dawes had alluded to in his after-action report. However, there is no evidence that Okey ever had possession of the colors. Dawes's report also noted that it had been Waller who had actually taken the colors.

Waller retained possession of his Medal, much to Okey's consternation, no doubt. Waller died in Bentford, South Dakota, on April 30, 1911. His remains were returned to De Soto, Wisconsin, where he was buried at the Walnut Mound Cemetery. Following his burial, his family donated his Medal, his war diary and other personal effects to the Vernon County Historical Society Museum in Viroqua, Wisconsin.

Considering the unusual challenges to Waller's ownership of the Medal, it should come as no surprise that in 1977, the museum reported the Medal stolen. No suspects in the theft were ever identified, and the Medal's whereabouts remained a mystery for fourteen years. Then, fortuitously, a collector in Ohio reached an oral agreement to purchase a collection of military medals from a New Hampshire antique dealer who was handling the estate of a nearby collector who had recently passed away. Before the deal could be consummated, however, the Ohio man read a book about the famous fight at the Railroad Cut in Gettysburg where Waller had earned the Medal of Honor. A footnote in the book noted that Waller's Medal had been stolen.

The Ohioan reported his discovery to the antique dealer, who in turn contacted the Viroqua police. Upon receiving confirmation that one of the medals in the collection was indeed Waller's Medal of Honor, the antique dealer reached out to the family of the man whose estate was being settled. The family, the antique dealer and the would-be purchaser of the Medal all agreed that the Medal should be returned to the museum, where it remains to this day. There is no record of how the collector in New Hampshire obtained the Medal.

Part IV

THE SECOND DAY OF BATTLE, JULY 2, 1863

Nathaniel M. Allen, Corporal, Company B, 1st Massachusetts Infantry

The son of a War of 1812 veteran, Nathaniel Allen had a spirit of patriotism instilled in him at a young age. Born on April 29, 1840, in Boston, he was working as a watchmaker when Fort Sumter was fired on to start the Civil War. When he learned that President Lincoln had issued a call for troops to defend the Union, he rushed to enlist. He was accepted into the 1st Massachusetts Infantry on May 22, 1861, a twenty-one-year-old private. Having impressed his officers with his abilities and attitude, he was promoted to corporal of the color guard, a rank he would hold until he mustered out in May 1864.

The Battle of Gettysburg had already concluded the first day of fighting when the 1st Massachusetts and the rest of Major General Andrew A. Humphreys's Division arrived well after dark near the Black Horse Tavern. The big problem? They were not where they were supposed to be, and now they were dangerously close to Rebel artillery. Poor directions had resulted in a wrong turn, and now the Union troops were inside Confederate lines. A captured Southern artillery sergeant revealed their exact whereabouts, and the Union troops left the area as silently as they could, not reaching their intended destination, the Round Top area, until 2:00 a.m.

Gravestone of Nathaniel Allen at Woodlawn Cemetery in Acton, Massachusetts. *Acton Historical Society, Acton, Massachusetts.*

After a restless night of sleep, the Bay Staters were placed on the extreme right of the Third Corps line along the west side of Emmitsburg Road the morning of July 2. In midafternoon, the Confederates assaulted the line repeatedly. During the fight, William Eaton, who was carrying the regiment's national flag, was wounded. The injured flag bearer passed the flag to the nearest man, who happened to be Allen.

Allen continued to carry the colors as the fighting grew more intense. Eventually, the 1st Massachusetts found itself hemmed in on three sides. When the left flank collapsed, the retreat rolled down the line, with the 1st Massachusetts joining in the move back to Cemetery Ridge.

During the retreat, Color Sergeant William Kelren, carrying the state flag, was shot and killed. As he fell, he dropped the flag, his lifeless body landing on top of it. Allen saw Kelren fall, and he turned back into the face of the assault. Disregarding the rapidly advancing Confederates and their heavy fire, he ran to the fallen colors and retrieved them from beneath Kelren's body. Now carrying both flags, he rushed to catch up with his retreating comrades and was able to carry both flags to safety. His quick reaction was credited with preventing the capture of the national colors.

On May 25, 1864, Allen mustered out and returned to his home in Boston, where he resumed working as a watchmaker. When his vision deteriorated to the point where he could no longer carry on his trade, he moved to South Acton, Massachusetts, where he lived with his sisters Adaline and Charlotte.

On July 2, 1899, the thirty-sixth anniversary of his actions to save the flag at Gettysburg, Allen was presented with the Medal of Honor after being nominated by his friends from Company B. The presentation took place at the regiment's reunion in Boston. His citation read:

> *When his regiment was falling back, this soldier, bearing the national color, returned in the face of the enemy's fire, pulled the regimental flag from under the body of its bearer, who had fallen, saved the flag from capture, and brought both colors off the field.*

On July 30, 1900, Allen died of nervous exhaustion and heart disease and was buried at Woodlawn Cemetery in South Acton. The town of South Acton dedicated a park in his memory, the Nathaniel Allen Recreation Area, on July 4, 2013.

John Barclay Fassett, Captain, Company F, 23rd Pennsylvania Infantry

It isn't often that a member of a regiment kept in reserve during a battle earns a Medal of Honor, but it happened for John Barclay Fassett.

The 23rd Pennsylvania, also known as Birney's Zouaves in honor of its commander, Major General David Birney, arrived on the Gettysburg battlefield on July 2 after an exhausting march of thirty-seven miles from Manchester, Maryland. Upon its arrival, it was placed on reserve just as Longstreet's Assault on Little Round Top was winding down. The men welcomed their brief respite, despite being in a position that kept them under fire.

Before the 23rd was settled in, Fassett, who was serving as senior aide to General Birney, was called on to assist in reforming Humphreys's Division after it had been forced back. As he was returning to report to General Birney, he spotted an officer from Battery I of the 5th United States Infantry sitting alone on a rock, staring toward the front lines. Curious as to why the man was not with his battery, Fassett approached him and was told that he no longer had a battery because it had been captured. The man then warned Fassett that if the Confederates got the battery's guns turned and aimed, it would be fully capable of decimating the troops that Fassett had just helped organize.

Fassett immediately saw that not only were Humphreys's troops in danger, but all of Cemetery Ridge would be endangered as well. With Cemetery Ridge being key to the Union position, Fassett immediately spurred his horse to the nearest Federal troops, the 39th New York, where he sought out the commanding officer and ordered him to retake the battery. When the officer asked Fassett who was giving the order, Fassett replied, "By order of General Birney."

When the officer replied that he wasn't under Birney's command and that he only took orders from General Hancock, Fassett retorted, "Then I order you to take the guns by order of General Hancock."

The officer heard the urgency in Fassett's command, and soon the New Yorkers were moving into position, from which they mounted a charge on the battery. As the only mounted officer, Fassett participated in the attack. And as the only mounted officer, Fassett became the best target.

John Barclay Fassett. *Congressional Medal of Honor Society, Mount Pleasant, South Carolina.*

When the Federals reached the battery, a Confederate immediately grabbed Fassett's horse's bridle. As Fassett struggled to release the man's grip, another Rebel raised his gun and fired directly at Fassett's face. Fortunately for Fassett, his reflexes were just fast enough, and as the man squeezed the trigger, Fassett swung his saber and struck the barrel of the gun, an action that undoubtedly saved his life. The ball passed through the brim of Fassett's kepi without touching him. Before the Confederate had time to reload, a member of the 39th New York killed him, sparing Fassett from further assault. When the battery was retaken, Fassett returned to his own line after commending the New Yorkers for their effort.

Fassett and the 23rd Pennsylvania Infantry would go on to fight at such battles as Mine Run, North Anna River, Cold Harbor, Petersburg and Weldon Railroad, among other smaller engagements, until they were mustered out on September 8, 1864. Fassett returned home to Philadelphia and resumed his life as a civilian.

On December 29, 1894, he was presented with the Medal of Honor, his citation saying in part:

> *While acting as an aide, voluntarily led a regiment to the relief of a battery and recaptured its gun from the enemy.*

Fassett died in Pasadena, California, on January 18, 1905, and was buried at Woodlawn Cemetery in Bronx, New York.

Charles Stacey, Private, Company D, 55th Ohio Infantry

Born in Cambridgeshire, England, on January 22, 1842, Charles Stacey came to the United States as a youth. Seeking adventure, he decided to enlist in the military service of his adopted country when the Civil War erupted. He signed on with Company D of the 55th Ohio Infantry on September 13, 1861, with his first battle being not against the Confederates but against a serious measles outbreak in February 1862 that killed an estimated twenty men of his regiment.

Over the next several months, Stacey and his comrades were present at a number of skirmishes and engagements, as well as the Battle of Cedar Mountain, but were held in reserve in all of them. Stacey would not get his first taste of combat until August 29, 1862, when they fought at the Second Battle of Bull Run, where the Union army was badly defeated. Stacey would not fight again until Chancellorsville, which resulted in another Union defeat.

By now Stacey and the rest of the 55th Ohio were tiring of the constant marching and the stinging defeats. On July 1, 1863, they arrived at the hamlet of Gettysburg, not knowing what to expect. At about 2:00 p.m., they formed a battle line behind a stone fence along Emmitsburg Road. With little activity in their area, the bored Ohioans watched gleefully as two men from an adjoining regiment came under fire from Confederate sharpshooters while carrying a kettle of coffee on a pole between them. The startled coffee bearers began to run, but one fell and the coffee kettle spilled its contents, to the delight of the men from Ohio. Seeing this, Stacey vowed that he would never become a source of amusement by showing fear under fire. The memory of that incident would garner him significant praise in the days to come.

On the second day of battle, Company D was ordered to take the place of skirmishers who had been driven back by unseen Rebel sharpshooters. Stacey volunteered to go outside the lines in an attempt to locate them. Working his way through a field of wheat, it didn't take Stacey long to find two, who spied him at the same time. Stacey disabled one of them with his first shot. He then engaged with the second sharpshooter for several minutes until the shooting from the sharpshooter's position stopped after Stacey's fourth shot.

The duel attracted the attention of the Confederate battle line along an old railroad cut, however, and each time Stacey fired his weapon at them he drew a volley from a company of sharpshooters, forcing him to take cover behind an old fence. Each round of fire showered him with splinters of wood from the fence rails, but he was able to effectively hide his actual position by crouching down into the surrounding wheat.

Charles Stacey. *Congressional Medal of Honor Society, Mount Pleasant, South Carolina.*

Sergeant L.B. Mesnard of Stacey's company saw the predicament his friend was in and made an attempt to reach him to lend assistance. However, when he was within about ten yards of Stacey's position, Stacey rose and fired once more, again drawing severe return fire. The volley caused wood splinters to be blown out of the fence into Mesnard's face, while the Confederate bullets also wounded him in the wrist and shattered his gun stock. The injured Mesnard, now with no weapon, was forced to retire and leave Stacey alone to continue his fight.

Alone, Stacey held his position for four hours, firing twenty-three shots over that time and driving the sharpshooters off with no injuries to anyone in his company except for Mesnard. Later that evening, Stacey was captured in a separate action. He remained a prisoner of war until May 19, 1864. After rejoining his regiment, he mustered out at the end of his enlistment on October 19, 1864.

On June 23, 1896, Stacey's heroism was recognized when he was presented with the Medal of Honor. His citation read, in part:

> *Voluntarily took an advanced position on the skirmish line for the purpose of ascertaining the location of Confederate sharpshooters and under heavy fire held the position thus taken until the company of which he was a member went back to the main line.*

Stacey died on October 17, 1924, at age eighty-two and was buried at Woodlawn Cemetery's mausoleum in Norwalk, Ohio.

George Washington Mears, Sergeant, Company A, 6th Pennsylvania Reserves

Wallace W. Johnson, Sergeant, Company G, 6th Pennsylvania Reserves

Chester S. Furman, Corporal, Company A, 6th Pennsylvania Reserves

John William Hart, Sergeant, Company D, 6th Pennsylvania Reserves

James Levi Roush, Corporal, Company D, 6th Pennsylvania Reserves

Thaddeus Stevens Smith, Corporal, Company E, 6th Pennsylvania Reserves

It is not common for six members of the same regiment to earn the Medal of Honor for the same action, but that is exactly what happened on July 2, 1863, at Gettysburg. On that date, Union forces had been forced back in ferocious fighting near Little Round Top.

As Federal reinforcements began to arrive, however, the Northerners began to stem the onslaught. At nearby Devil's Den, the Union troops were still coming under heavy fire from an unknown location. After some time, it was determined that Confederate sharpshooters in a small log house about half a mile from Devil's Den were the source. Although no longer there, the house sat on land adjacent to a future farmhouse known as the John Weikert farmhouse, which was built after the war. Their heavy and accurate fire was taking a deadly toll on the Union troops.

Recognizing the need for the firing from the log house to be eliminated, the 6th Pennsylvania Reserves' (aka the 35th Pennsylvania Volunteer infantry) Colonel W. Wallace Ricketts sent a runner to brigade commander Colonel William McCandless of the 2nd Reserves, saying that the 6th Reserves were at his disposal. When McCandless agreed to have Ricketts's men silence the Rebel sharpshooters, Ricketts called for volunteers.

Six men stepped forward: Sergeant George Washington Mears and Corporal Chester S. Furman of Company A, Sergeant John William Hart

Left: George Washington Mears. *Congressional Medal of Honor Society, Mount Pleasant, South Carolina.*

Right: Wallace W. Johnson. *Congressional Medal of Honor Society, Mount Pleasant, South Carolina.*

and Corporal James Levi Roush of Company D, Corporal Thaddeus Stevens Smith of Company E and Sergeant Wallace W. Johnson of Company G.

After a brief discussion of how they would make their assault, the six began a stealthy advance on the cabin, taking advantage of the smoke of battle to conceal their movement. Before they had gone half the distance to the cabin, someone inside the structure noticed them and sounded the alarm. Now the fire was no longer directed at the brigade. The sharpshooters inside the cabin focused their attention on the six men slowly making their way to their stronghold.

The six attackers immediately changed their tactic from one of stealth to one of racing toward the cabin en masse. Miraculously, they all reached the log house unscathed. Once there they knocked down the door and leveled their weapons on those inside, demanding their surrender. The demeanor of the attacking Federals made it plain that they were not going to negotiate and that the options were limited. To a man, the sharpshooters dropped their weapons and surrendered to their assailants. The Confederates were marched back to the Union line amid cheers from the Federals.

The six would see their own fates differ as the war drew to its eventual close. Mears was badly wounded at New Hope Church on November 27,

Left: Chester S. Furman. *Congressional Medal of Honor Society, Mount Pleasant, South Carolina.*

Right: James Levi Roush. *Hall of Valor.*

1863, and was in the hospital when his comrades mustered out the following summer. Hart, Johnson and Roush mustered out on July 11, 1864, while Smith and Furman transferred to other units, Smith to the 191st Pennsylvania Volunteers and Furman to the U.S. Signal Corps.

All six eventually received the Medal of Honor for their daring attack, but for some reasons at varying times. Roush, Furman and Hart were the first to receive theirs on August 3, 1897. Smith received his on May 5, 1900, and Johnson his on August 3, 1897. Mears would have to wait until February 16, 1907, to become the last of the six to be so honored. Roush, Furman, Hart and Smith had the same wording on their citations:

> *Was one of six volunteers who charged upon a log house near the Devil's Den, where a squad of the enemy's sharpshooters were sheltered, and compelled their surrender.*

For unknown reasons, Mears's and Johnson's citations were slightly different:

> *With five other volunteers gallantly charged on a number of the enemy's sharpshooters concealed in a log house, captured them, and brought them into the Union lines.*

6th Pennsylvania Reserves Monument, from where John William Hart, Thaddeus Stevens Smith and four of their companions launched their assault on the log cabin. *Author photo.*

Although the last to receive his Medal, Mears was the first to die, passing away on November 24, 1891. He was buried at Old Rosemont Cemetery in Bloomsburg, Pennsylvania. Roush was the second, passing away on February 12, 1906. He was buried at the New St. Patrick's Cemetery in Newry, Pennsylvania. He was followed by Hart, who died on June 12, 1908, and was laid to rest at St. Luke's Trinity Lutheran Cemetery in Cumberland, Maryland, followed by Furman, who died on July 22, 1910, and was interred near Mears at the same cemetery in Bloomsburg. Johnson followed the next year on December 30, 1911, with his burial taking place at West Laurel Hill Cemetery in Bala Cynwyd, Pennsylvania. The last of the six, Smith, took his last breath on March 14, 1933, and was buried at Laurel Grove Cemetery in Port Townsend, Washington.

Thomas Horan, Sergeant, Company E, 72nd New York Infantry

The family of Thomas Horan, born in Ireland in 1839 to Michael and Mary Horan, was suffering greatly from the Great Famine. When Thomas was about nine years old, he moved with his parents and younger brother Michael to the United States, settling in Dunkirk, New York. When the Civil War began, Thomas, as did many Irish immigrants, enlisted in the Union army. He was mustered into the 72nd New York Volunteers on May 14, 1861, as a private. He was promoted to corporal eight months later and to sergeant in September 1862. The regiment would become known as the Third Excelsior Regiment, serving in the famed Excelsior Brigade.

By the time it got to Gettysburg, the regiment had developed a reputation for being excellent fighters, having been tested at such battles as Williamsburg, Seven Pines, Malvern Hill, Brawner Farm, Second Bull Run, Fredericksburg and Chancellorsville. The regiment had already lost five officers killed or mortally wounded plus another ninety-six enlisted men. There would be more to come before the regiment mustered out.

The regiment arrived at Gettysburg long after nightfall on July 1, 1863. The first day's battle had already concluded, and the field was silent except for the occasional gunfire, usually from nervous pickets shooting at shadows. The men settled in for what would be a very restless and broken sleep. They had heard about the vicious fighting that had taken place earlier that day. They knew that it would start all over again tomorrow and that they would be a part of it this time.

The Excelsior Brigade monument, which included the 72nd New York, sits in the area where Thomas Horan captured the flag of the 8th Florida Infantry. *Author photo.*

Shortly after noon on July 2, the regiment went into position with the rest of the Excelsior Brigade along Emmitsburg Road. They it moved forward toward Joseph Sherfy's peach orchard, where it endured heavy artillery fire for more than an hour. When the barrage ended, the Confederates attacked, and soon the New Yorkers found themselves embroiled in a devastating battle. Forced to retreat with the rest of the Third Corps, they took heavy casualties, including the wounding of the 72nd's commander, Colonel John Austin.

Reorganizing near the foot of Little Round Top, Horan and his companions prepared for the next assault, which came not long after. However, by now fresh troops had come as reinforcements, and this time the line held. Once again the fighting was ferocious, and eventually the fatigued Confederates began to drop back. Taking command, Horan led the 72nd New York in a pursuit of the Rebels.

When the Southerners—which happened to be Brigadier General Edward Perry's Brigade, made up of the 2nd, 5th and 8th Florida Infantries—stopped to take a stand, the men of the 72nd New York found themselves facing the 8th Florida. Horan, in the lead, raced for the flag bearer of the

8th Florida. While records of exactly what transpired are sketchy, it is known that the flag bearer was wounded, perhaps mortally, and that Horan gained control of his flag.

The next day, July 3, the 8th Florida took part in Pickett's Charge, minus its flag and flag bearer. For their part, the 72nd New York and the rest of the Excelsior Brigade supported the left center of the Union line in the assault.

Horan was seriously wounded at the Battle of the Wilderness on May 7, 1864, rendering him unable to muster out with his regiment six weeks later. He survived his wound and returned to Dunkirk, New York. On April 5, 1898, his bravery was rewarded when he was presented with the Medal of Honor. His citation summarizes his actions as follows:

> *In a charge of his regiment this soldier captured the regimental flag of the 8th Florida Infantry (C.S.A.).*

Horan eventually moved to Madison, Illinois, where he died in 1902 at age sixty-three. His remains were returned to Dunkirk, where he was buried at St. Mary's Cemetery.

Richard Enderlin, Musician, Company B, 73rd Ohio Infantry

Richard Enderlin lay in the dark, trying to shut out the cries and moans of the wounded still unattended out beyond the line. Some called for their mothers, and others called out the name of a sweetheart or spouse. Union, Confederate—they all sounded the same when they were in pain. The cries weren't as loud as they had been previously, nor were there as many, but that was of little consolation to Enderlin. That probably only meant one thing: there were fewer still alive.

Enderlin was born in Baden, Germany, on January 11, 1843, but had come to the United States as a child, growing up in Chillicothe, Ohio. As with many other soldiers who fought in the Union army, he had wanted to fight for his adopted country when the Civil War broke out, and in November 1861, he enlisted in the 73rd Ohio Infantry as a musician. He was made the regiment's bugler.

Upon arrival at Gettysburg around noon on July 1, 1863, the regiment was assigned a position on East Cemetery Hill. There, it rested for several hours. Enderlin couldn't help but reflect on those souls already buried there, wondering if he would be among them by nightfall. Over the next twenty-four hours, the regiment moved to several positions, eventually being relieved each time without engaging in the fighting except for the occasional sporadic fire.

After only a few hours' sleep, the regiment was awakened at 3:00 a.m. on July 2 and moved to Taneytown Road, with orders to protect the artillery on East Cemetery Hill. At midafternoon, after a morning of ominous silence, Confederate artillery opened a prolonged barrage, answered by the Union batteries. The 73rd Ohio Infantry found itself to be in what appeared to be the center of the target of the Rebel guns; it was also coming under fire from sharpshooters in the town itself. Enderlin, seeing the danger the regiment was in, picked up the rifle of a fallen soldier and joined in the fight.

Richard Enderlin. *Congressional Medal of Honor Society, Mount Pleasant, South Carolina.*

Now it was dark, and Enderlin and his friends were trying to sleep, but with little success. The crack of skirmishers' guns sporadically broke through the night. He was used to hearing gunfire and had slept through it many times before, so that wasn't keeping him awake. Now it was those screams of pain from the wounded. They never stopped.

Somewhere out there between the two lines was his friend, Private George Nixon. Nixon had been wounded earlier in the day, before the regiment had dropped back, and Enderlin hadn't seen him since. The bugler hoped that his friend was one of those moaning. It would mean he was still alive. He wondered why the officers wouldn't call a truce long enough for each side to bring in the wounded? He also contemplated gathering some friends to search for George and the rest of the regiment's wounded, but he knew that such a move would be suicidal. In the darkness, they would most likely draw fire from both sides.

He then considered doing it himself. Almost immediately he talked himself out of that plan, but the thought never went away. Each time he considered it, it seemed to be more possible. And he knew that George would do it for him. Finally, he decided that every minute he waited made George's chance of survival a bit less likely. Without a word, he slipped across the line and began moving forward on his belly, propelling himself forward with his feet and elbows.

As he reached the area where the regiment had been earlier in the day, he began his search. Calling his friend's name softly, he finally got a response. Within seconds, he was beside George, and even in the darkness he could see that he had been wounded badly, once in the right hip and once in the right side. George was only semiconscious and couldn't move under his own power. Enderlin knew that he would have to either drag or carry George back to the Union line.

Grabbing his friend under one arm, he began the laborious rescue. He soon found that he couldn't get much leverage and knew he couldn't continue that way. He rolled Nixon onto his side and then crawled under him and rolled him onto his own back. Carrying Nixon on his back made his movements easier, but as he feared, it wasn't long until he was spotted. Shots rang out, first from the Confederates and then from the Union side. He couldn't be sure if they were shooting at him or each other, but it didn't matter. The balls were zipping past his head, and he ducked reflexively each time, even though he knew the deadly missile was already long past him.

Occasionally taking cover behind a prone body long enough to catch his breath, he slowly brought George Nixon toward friendly faces. Finally, after what seemed an eternity, he got close enough to the line to identify himself and bring his friend to safety.

Nixon was taken to the George Spangler farm for treatment, but despite Enderlin's heroics, he did not survive. Nixon was buried on the Spangler farm before being moved to the Ohio section of Gettysburg National Cemetery later. Fifty years later, his great-grandson was born. Richard Milhous Nixon would go on to become the thirty-seventh president of the United States. As vice president, Nixon visited Gettysburg several times, making it a point to stop at the cemetery to pay respects to his great-grandfather.

For his heroics, Enderlin was promoted to sergeant the next day. He remained the bugler for the 73rd Ohio until he was wounded at the Battle of Dallas (Georgia) on May 28, 1864. He was discharged as a result of his wound.

He returned to Chillicothe, and on September 11, 1897, he was awarded the Medal of Honor. His citation tells the story:

> *Voluntarily took a rifle and served as a soldier in the ranks during the first and second days of the battle. Voluntarily and at his own imminent peril went into the enemy's lines at night and, under a sharp fire, rescued a wounded comrade.*

Thirty-three years later, on the cold winter morning of February 11, 1930, Richard Enderlin passed away in his home in Chillicothe. He was buried at Grandview Cemetery in Chillicothe

Joshua Chamberlain, Colonel, 20th Maine Infantry

Anyone who has seen the movie *Gettysburg* knows the story of Joshua Chamberlain. Born in Brewer, Maine, on September 8, 1828, to Joshua Chamberlain and Sarah Dupee, he came by his military prowess naturally. His great-grandfather had served in both the French and Indian War and the Revolutionary War, his grandfather had served in the War of 1812 and his father had served in the Aroostook War, a dispute between the United States and the United Kingdom in 1838–39 over the boundary between the state of Maine and the British colony of New Brunswick.

Chamberlain, who eventually was fluent in French, Arabic, Hebrew and Syriac, was also able to speak Latin and German at a less fluent level. He also taught himself Greek because he needed the language to be admitted to Bowdoin College, from which he graduated in 1852.

He became an instructor at his alma mater and then became a professor of rhetoric and oratory. He felt strongly that the southern states were wrong in wishing to leave the Union, and when he was granted a leave of absence to study in Europe, he chose to enlist as the lieutenant colonel of the 20th Maine Infantry. He became colonel in June 1863 when the regiment's commander, Colonel Adelbert Ames, was promoted.

Joshua Chamberlain. *Congressional Medal of Honor Society, Mount Pleasant, South Carolina.*

One month earlier, while still a lieutenant colonel, he became involved in an incident that figured prominently in the 20th Maine's fight at Gettysburg. With no hint that there would even be a battle at Gettysburg, 120 men from the 2nd Maine Infantry were brought under guard to the 20th Maine's encampment. The 120 men had enlisted for a three-year service but had become enraged when most of their regiment, made up of men who had signed up for two-year enlistments, had been discharged, with the regiment disbanded. Those left behind refused to fight for any other regiment, despite still having another year to go in their own enlistments.

Chamberlain was given orders to shoot any of those who refused duty. He first talked to the men and heard their complaint and then offered them the opportunity to serve with the 20th Maine. He was able to convince them that he would treat them fairly, and when they agreed, he wisely distributed them throughout the regiment's companies. This move served two purposes. It separated men who had a common complaint, serving to reduce the potential for another mutiny, and it also placed experienced combat veterans with the relatively inexperienced men of the 20th, bringing his regiment's strength up to 386 men. These additional forces would prove invaluable at Gettysburg.

The regiment was placed on the extreme left flank of the Union line on Little Round Top on July 2, 1863, with orders to hold that position at all costs. Failure to hold could mean the folding of the entire Union line. This dramatic order set the stage for Chamberlain's heroics.

Late in the afternoon, troops from the 15th Alabama, under Colonel William Oates, assaulted the Mainers' position. The Alabamans had arrived on the battlefield at the end of a twenty-five-mile march in the July heat and were pressed into service almost immediately. Tired, hot and with no water, they rushed up the slope to the 20th Maine's position, only to be pushed back.

The Southerners attacked several times, with Chamberlain's men pushing them back each time and holding the line. The 47th Alabama soon joined in the fight. However, after a three-hour fight, the Maine troops still held, nearly out of ammunition. The end of their line, the *real* extreme left of the Union line, had nearly doubled back on itself. Chamberlain realized that the situation called for desperate action.

Historians debate what happened next. Some say it was Chamberlain who ordered the famous bayonet charge, some say another officer and some believe that it happened spontaneously. However it happened, Chamberlain is credited. The 20th Maine made its charge down the hill, with the left flank of his line swinging around like a gate. This had the effect of flanking the 15th Alabama with part of his regiment while at the same time inflicting a frontal assault with the rest. The unexpected move caught the Alabamans by surprise. When it appeared that the Rebels might be able to fight off the assault, Chamberlain's Company B rose from its position behind a stone wall and fired a volley into the unsuspecting Confederate rear. The ensuing confusion and panic had the effect of ending the fight. The 20th Maine's monument indicates that it took 308 prisoners.

Chamberlain and the 20th Maine went on to fight in several more battles. At the Second Battle of Petersburg, he was shot through the hip and groin, a wound that the surgeons believed was mortal. Lieutenant General Ulysses Grant gave him a promotion to brigadier general on the recommendation from Fifth Corps commander Gouverneur Warren, who suggested the promotion before Chamberlain could pass. Surprisingly, Chamberlain survived his wound, although it plagued him the rest of his life.

He returned to become a brigade commander in the Fifth Corps and was wounded once again at the Quaker Road, a wound that nearly necessitated the amputation of his left arm.

On April 9, 1965, Robert E. Lee surrendered at Appomattox. Chamberlain was selected to preside over the parade of the Confederate army as part of the surrender ceremony. As the defeated Southerners marched solemnly past, Chamberlain ordered his men to attention and place their weapons in the "carry arms" position as a show of respect. Seeing this, Confederate General John Gordon returned the salute by having the Confederates respond in kind.

Chamberlain's war record showed that he fought in twenty battles, was cited for bravery four times, was wounded six times and had six horses shot from under him. Following the war, he served as governor of Maine and then returned to Bowdoin College as its president. He would undergo six surgeries to repair his original wound. None was completely successful.

On August 11, 1893, he received the Medal of Honor, accompanied by the citation, which read in part:

> *Daring heroism and great tenacity in holding his position on the Little Round Top against repeated assaults, and carrying the advance position on the Great Round Top.*

The effects of his wounds finally caught up with him, and he died on February 24, 1914, in Portland, Maine, of complications from those wounds. He was the last Civil War veteran to die as a result of his wounds. He was buried at Pine Grove Cemetery in Brunswick, Maine.

The 1896 version of his Medal is in the Joshua L. Chamberlain Museum in Brunswick, Maine, while the 1904 version is in the Hawthorne-Longfellow Library at Bowdoin College, also in Brunswick.

Andrew Jackson Tozier, Sergeant, Company I, 20th Maine Infantry

While Colonel Joshua Chamberlain's actions on Little Round Top were certainly heroic, as described, he was not the only member of the 20th Maine to perform in such fashion on July 2, 1863. The regiment's flag bearer, Andrew Jackson Tozier, proved to be every bit as brave and made a name for himself in much the same fashion as did his commanding officer.

Tozier was born in Monmouth, Maine, on February 11, 1838. He ran away from home in his early teens to get away from an abusive family life, and he is believed to have become a sailor on a merchant ship. At the age of twenty-three, he returned home but didn't stay long, enlisting in the 2nd Maine Infantry in July 1861. Promoted to corporal early in 1862, he was wounded and captured in his first battle, the Battle of Gaines' Mill. There, he was shot in the ankle and through a finger, with the finger being amputated by a Confederate surgeon the next day. Sent to Belle Isle prison in the middle of the James River at Richmond, he was paroled just a few weeks later and returned home to recuperate. Once healed sufficiently, he rejoined his regiment.

In May 1863, Tozier was one of the 120 members of the 2nd Maine Infantry who mutinied when the bulk of their regiment was sent home when their two-year enlistment ended. This incident is described in greater detail in the previous account for Colonel Chamberlain. Along with his 119 comrades from the 2nd Maine Infantry, Tozier was placed under arrest and marched under guard to Chamberlain's 20th Maine camp. There they met with Chamberlain, who was under orders to shoot any one of them who refused duty. Either Chamberlain's persuasive discussion or the threat of being shot had the desired effect, and the men from the 2nd Maine Infantry became part of the 20th Maine, with Tozier being assigned to Company I.

Just three weeks later, the 20th Maine's color bearer was placed under arrest for being drunk while on the march, and Tozier, being the senior enlisted man, was made the color sergeant for his new regiment.

On July 2, as described previously, the regiment was on the extreme left flank of the Union line, with orders to hold its position at all costs. Facing the 15th Alabama Infantry and later, the 47th Alabama Infantry, he stood firm in front of the line. With bullets whizzing past him, he stood upright and held his flag defiantly, seeming to dare the Alabamans to come and take it. The sight of him standing tall in the face of the attack was later said to be the rallying point for the center of the line to hold, and they

20th Maine monument. From this approximate position, flag bearer Andrew Tozier led the regiment's bayonet charge. *Author photo.*

did. Some accounts say that he held his flag with one hand and fired his weapon with the other.

When the regiment made the famous bayonet charge down the slope, Tozier and Lieutenant Holman Melcher led the charge, with the rest following behind the colors. When the fighting was over, Tozier was credited with being the spark that inspired the Mainers to continue fighting.

Tozier was wounded again at the Battle of North Anna on May 26, 1864, with the wound nearly ending his life. The bullet entered his head just behind the eye, and most of it exited before penetrating into the brain. With a portion still lodged in his skull, Tozier continued to serve until he mustered out on July 15, 1864.

Returning to civilian life, Tozier, unfortunately, embarked on a crime spree with his half brother, stealing cattle and robbing a clothing store. The spree lasted, sporadically, until 1869, when he was finally brought to justice. Pleading guilty to the clothing store robbery, he was sentenced to five years at hard labor in the state penitentiary. Fortunately for Tozier, he was not there long, receiving a pardon from the governor for all his crimes.

That governor? None other than Tozier's old colonel, Joshua Chamberlain, who invited Tozier and his family to live with the Chamberlain family, an arrangement that was successful for several years until Tozier returned to Monmouth and tried dairy farming. The lingering effects of his wounds, however, proved to be too much, and he could not continue that endeavor. He then worked at a rake and broom factory and became active in the local post of the Grand Army of the Republic.

In 1898, Chamberlain wrote a letter to the War Department recommending Tozier for the Medal of Honor. That recommendation was approved, and the Medal was awarded on August 13, 1898. The Medal was sent to his home via parcel post. His citation read:

> *At the crisis of the engagement this soldier, a color bearer, stood alone in an advanced position, the regiment having been borne back, and defended his colors with musket and ammunition picked up at his feet.*

The Medal was believed to be lost later in a fire that destroyed his son's home in Farmingdale, Maine.

Andrew Jackson Tozier died on March 28, 1910, and was buried at Litchfield Plains Cemetery in Litchfield, Maine.

Edward M. Knox, Second Lieutenant, 15th Battery, New York Light Artillery

Edward Knox was born on February 12, 1842, in New York City, and it was only natural that he would enlist in a New York regiment when the Civil War began. He chose the 15th New York Light Artillery when it was being organized in late 1862.

On July 2, 1863, Knox found himself in Gettysburg, a small town he had never heard of before. The battery had just been ordered to a position in a small peach orchard that belonged to the Reverend Joseph Sherfy. The Sherfy farm sat across Emmitsburg Road, and across the fields sat the Confederate artillery.

Knox set up his guns and began firing, with the Confederates doing the same. An intense but relatively short artillery duel ensued, with the Rebels withdrawing. But Knox and his men could not relax, as a line of infantry was advancing toward him. Knox fired his guns directly into the assault, driving the Confederates back. Once reorganized, the Rebels launched another assault, which the New Yorkers repulsed once again. A third effort was also slowed, but by now Knox was getting low on ammunition.

As the Rebel line advanced toward his guns, he fired one last volley of double canister, opening up a huge hole in the gray line. Then, with no time to reload, he yelled to his gunners to throw themselves to the ground as if shot and to remain prone until the Rebels had passed. His men complied, and the advancing troops passed over them without giving the "dead" gun crew a second glance.

Edward M. Knox. *Congressional Medal of Honor Society, Mount Pleasant, South Carolina.*

The Confederate attack continued until it reached Union infantry behind Knox's guns, where the Federal line held. Soon, the Southerners returned, this time in full retreat. Knox and his men had remained on the ground, and once again, the Rebel infantry passed over them. Once they had passed, Knox rose to his feet and only then realized that his guns were the only ones still in position.

Still under fire, he and his crew began pulling the guns back by hand, working their way around the dead and wounded. In the process, Knox was badly wounded but continued to help haul the guns back to prevent their capture. By the time the 15th Light Artillery was finished, Knox's battery had lost seven men and eleven horses.

The next day, while defending the Union line during Pickett's Charge, Knox received a second severe wound, this time being shot through both hips. He would spend the next eighteen months in various hospitals as an invalid. Although he was promoted to first lieutenant, he was never physically able to resume his service.

His action on July 2 was credited with saving the guns, and on October 18, 1892, those actions were rewarded when he was presented with the Medal of Honor. The accompanying citation stated:

> *Held his ground with the battery after the other batteries had fallen back until compelled to draw his piece off by hand; he was severely wounded.*

Edward Knox died in New York on March 28, 1916, and was buried at Woodlawn Cemetery in the Bronx.

Harrison Clark, Corporal, Company E, 125th New York Infantry

Born on April 10, 1842, in Chatham, New York, Harrison Clark worked as a carriage maker before the Civil War began. When he learned that a new regiment was being formed in Troy, New York, just thirty miles away, he set out to become a soldier. There, he mustered into the 125th New York Infantry on August 12, 1862.

One month later, he surrendered with the garrison on September 15 while in defense of Harper's Ferry, the regiment's first official action. He wasn't a prisoner very long, however, being paroled the next day and sent to Camp Douglas in Chicago to guard prisoners until his official exchange, which came on September 22, 1862.

After briefly participating in the defense of Washington, Clark and his regiment were relatively inactive until June 25, 1863, when they left camp at Centerville, Virginia, and marched northward, arriving in Gettysburg on the morning of July 2.

At about 7:00 p.m. that same day, the Union left was under attack by Confederate General William Barksdale's Mississippi Brigade. The 125th New York was ordered to go to the Plum Run area to lend support to the Federal line. The troops reached their assigned location with the rest of the brigade, comprising the 39th, 111th and 126th New York in addition to themselves, but could only make out shapes of men moving around. Believing them to be the advancing Rebels, the entire brigade opened fire, only to hear the command to cease fire—they were shooting into the Union ranks.

Harrison Clark. *Congressional Medal of Honor Society, Mount Pleasant, South Carolina.*

Not long after, Colonel George L. Willard gave the order to attack. As the regiment began its advance, it was immediately met with a volley from the approaching Mississippians, killing the color bearer and most of the color guard. Without the colors to follow, the regiment was in danger of being routed.

Seeing the color bearer go down, Clark rushed to catch the flag before it dropped. He then led the charge into the oncoming Confederates, with men from both sides being killed or wounded in huge numbers. According to Second Lieutenant Harry

Haskell, acting adjutant for the regiment, the losses to the Federals were becoming so heavy that Colonel Willard ordered the entire brigade to fall back. The colonel was killed shortly after.

Reaching a small swale, the regiment reformed amid the bodies of more than one hundred Union men from the brigade. The regiment began a slow withdrawal to its original position near East Cemetery Hill. Clark was singled out by the officers for the bravery he had shown in the fight, and he was given a field promotion to the rank of sergeant and made the official color bearer.

The next day, as Pickett's Charge began to fall apart, Clark jumped over the stone wall that had offered the Union line a bit of protection. Rushing forward, he followed the retreating attackers, who turned and fired at him. When he reached the safety of a small board fence, he noticed that the flag had received fifteen bullet holes.

Clark escaped injury at Gettysburg and subsequent engagements until May 6, 1864. At the Battle of the Wilderness, he led another charge, getting to within ten feet of the enemy line when a bullet shattered his leg. Lieutenant Colonel Aaron B. Myer, temporarily in command of the regiment, assisted in binding his wound and promoted Clark to second lieutenant on the field as he rested. His leg was later amputated. He would never be mustered in as a lieutenant, however, before he was discharged while at the Ira Harris Hospital in Albany on September 4, 1865.

As Clark fell, the flag was grabbed by Private Philip Brady of Company I, who was killed within minutes as he moved the banner forward.

After being released from medical care, Clark returned home and married Harriett Emeline Johnson, and the two had three children. Clark became the proprietor of an opera house and later became keeper of the Bureau of Military Services.

On June 11, 1895, Clark was awarded the Medal of Honor for his actions in saving the flag and leading the regimental charge at Gettysburg. According to his citation, he:

Seized the colors and advanced with them after the color bearer had been shot.

Clark died on April 18, 1913, and his remains were interred at the Albany Rural Cemetery in Albany, New York.

Casper R. Carlisle, Private, Battery F, Independent Pennsylvania Light Artillery

Casper Carlisle was born in Allegheny County, Pennsylvania, sometime in 1841. Little is known of his early years, but it is known that he joined Battery F of the Independent Pennsylvania Light Artillery at age nineteen. He was officially mustered for a three-year commitment.

The battery was mustered in on October 8, 1861, and had already seen significant action before getting to Gettysburg, having fought at Hancock, Winchester, Sulphur Springs, Second Bull Run, Chantilly, Antietam and Chancellorsville. Just before arriving in Gettysburg, the battery was consolidated with Battery C due to heavy casualties suffered by both batteries. The commanding officer for the batteries was Captain James Thompson, and the combined batteries fought as part of Freeman McGilvery's 1st Volunteer Artillery Brigade.

On July 2, 1863, Battery F, also known as Hampton's Battery, moved into the Peach Orchard at Gettysburg. Without orders to do so, General Daniel Sickles moved his Third Corps troops off Cemetery Ridge to the Peach Orchard, believing that ground offered a better defensive position. The battery was part of a solid line of fifty-eight cannons placed in support of Sickles, four of Battery F's aimed in the direction of the nearby Rose farm and the other two aimed toward Seminary Ridge to the west.

Late in the afternoon, General James Longstreet launched his assault. South Carolina troops under General Joseph Kershaw had come across the Rose farm, and the artillery had done devastating work on the Southerners' left flank as they passed. Then came General William Barksdale's Mississippians, who did much the same to Sickles.

Sickles's line finally collapsed and was forced back. The Confederate onslaught threatened to overrun the batteries, and as they got closer, they began to shoot the horses to prevent the removal of the guns. If the Confederates could capture the guns, they would turn them and use them against the Federal troops, inflicting untold damage on the retreating line. Recognizing the danger, Carlisle resisted the urge to retreat to a safer area and stood his ground. As the Rebel line neared the line of cannons, the intensity of the fighting grew. Carlisle scrambled to get his few remaining horses in position, and with several Confederates shooting at him from what seemed to him like point-blank range, he was able to get his gun safely to the rear. In the fight at the Peach Orchard, the battery had fourteen men killed or wounded and lost eighteen horses. Carlisle somehow escaped unscathed.

Casper R. Carlisle saved a battery gun from capture near the regiment's monument in the Peach Orchard. *Author photo.*

He would go on to reenlist for another three-year term of enlistment in February 1864 but would muster out on June 26, 1865, following Lee's surrender. On December 21, 1892, Carlisle's bravery was officially recognized when he was presented with the Medal of Honor. The accompanying citation read:

> *Saved a gun of his battery under heavy musketry fire, most of the horses being killed and the drivers wounded.*

On April 29, 1908, Casper Carlisle died and was buried at Mount Lebanon Cemetery in Pittsburgh.

CHARLES WELLINGTON REED, BUGLER, 9TH INDEPENDENT BATTERY, MASSACHUSETTS LIGHT ARTILLERY

Charles Wellington Reed was born on March 1, 1842, in Charlestown, Massachusetts. His family was relatively wealthy, and Charles was able to attend several private schools to study art. It would become his passion.

When it appeared as if there was going to be a civil war, Reed enrolled in a local militia known as Salignac's Zouaves, where he aspired to learn military drill. On August 2, 1862, with the Civil War well underway, he enlisted in the 9th Independent Battery, Massachusetts Light Artillery, or the 9th Massachusetts Light Artillery, as it was more commonly called. He became the battery's bugler, although he worked to gain a staff appointment. As a sideline, he sketched what he saw as a soldier, including camp life, marches, battles and ceremonies.

On July 2, 1863, the battery, under the command of Captain John Bigelow, occupied a position along Wheatfield Road as part of the fifty-eight-gun line described previously. The battery had never been in battle, and the reality that it was now going to happen made Reed nervous.

The battery fired on Confederate batteries along Emmitsburg Road and on troops around the Rose farm. When Kershaw's Brigade began moving across the fields in front of the battery, the Bay Staters fired with canister as rapidly as they could, causing significant damage to the Southern line.

By 6:00 p.m., the battery found itself alone on the line after the collapse of Sickles's Corps. It was forced to retreat by prolonge firing, meaning the guns had to be pulled by the men using their prolonges, or ropes with hooks attached. As they pulled the cannons backward, they stopped periodically to fire. They used this technique until they reached the Trostle farm, where they took another stand without support.

In the fighting, Reed's role as bugler was to sound the bugle calls that directed the actions of the men. He also fired a weapon as he was able. In the retreat, Captain Bigelow was badly wounded, falling between the retreating battery and the advancing Confederates. Under constant fire, Reed grabbed

Charles Reed's heroics in rescuing Captain John Bigelow in the regiment's retreat to this position at the Trostle farm earned him the Medal of Honor. *Author photo.*

the reins of his horse and another one whose rider had been a casualty. Leading the two horses toward the oncoming Rebel line, he lifted Bigelow onto one of the horses and mounted the second one himself. He then led Bigelow to safety and prevented his death or capture.

Reed would go on to fight at the Battle of the Wilderness, Spotsylvania Court House and the Siege of Petersburg, where he suffered a serious wound to his right hand from a Rebel saber. In November 1864, he was finally able to attain the staff position he had long coveted when he was assigned to General Gouverneur K. Warren's staff as a topographical engineer. He was selected for the position based on his prolific sketching that produced more than seven hundred drawings of army life. His sketches were used extensively in the 1887 book *Hardtack and Coffee* by John Billings.

Following the war, Reed became an artist and illustrator as a profession, contributing his work to the *Boston Globe*. He also opened a studio, where he painted landscapes and portraits.

On August 16, 1895, based on Bigelow's recommendation, Reed was awarded the Medal of Honor, with the citation saying:

Rescued his wounded captain from between the lines.

Reed died in Norwell, Massachusetts, on April 29, 1926, and was interred at Mount Auburn Cemetery in Cambridge, Massachusetts. His Medal is now in the Manuscript Division (Charles Wellington Papers) at the Library of Congress.

James Jackson Purman, First Lieutenant, Company A, 140th Pennsylvania Infantry

James Milton Pipes, Captain, Company A, 140th Pennsylvania Infantry

Another dramatic rescue was taking place on another part of the battlefield that same day that involved two young men who lived not far apart in their civilian life. The two would earn the Medal of Honor together, although one of these men would have a second heroic action at a later date added to his citation.

James Jackson Purman was born on a farm near Waynesburg, in Greene County, Pennsylvania, in 1841. While attending Waynesburg College, the ambitious Purman also had a teaching job at a local school, as well as a typesetting job at the local newspaper, a job he had held since age twelve.

Frustrated at the number of battlefield defeats the Union army was experiencing, he decided to join with three friends to start their own volunteer cavalry corps. The first to sign up was a young man named James Pipes, who joined on August 18, 1862. Pipes, less than a year older than Purman, would join with Purman at Gettysburg to perform a rescue that earned both of them the Medal of Honor.

With the Union army no longer accepting volunteer cavalry units, the newly minted group called themselves the Greene County Rifles and took a riverboat to Pittsburgh to muster in with the 140th Pennsylvania Infantry. The regiment's first assignment was guarding a railroad near Parkton, Maryland, followed by their first battle action at Chancellorsville on May 2, 1863, where the regiment gave a good account of itself in pushing back several Confederate attacks.

The regiment saw no additional action until July 2, 1863. Under the command of Colonel R.P. Roberts, the regiment arrived at Gettysburg that morning. At about 4:00 p.m., it was ordered to assist the Third Corps near

Left: James Jackson Purman. *Congressional Medal of Honor Society, Mount Pleasant, South Carolina.*

Right: James Milton Pipes. *Congressional Medal of Honor Society, Mount Pleasant, South Carolina.*

an area known today as the Loop. The 140th PVI formed up on the extreme right of the battle line. On the given order, the men opened fire and began to advance into the Wheatfield.

Shortly after reaching a small crest of a hill, fresh Confederate troops began to outflank the right of the Federal line, which was the 140th Pennsylvania. The extreme left of the line began to collapse, triggering a rolling retreat along the line toward the Pennsylvanians. By now, Colonel Roberts had been killed, and Lieutenant Colonel John Fraser ordered the regiment to hold as long as it could. When it was apparent that it was no longer possible to continue the fight, the troops began an orderly withdrawal, stopping several times to fire against their pursuers.

In the retreat, Purman and Pipes saw Company C's Private John Buckley crying for help. The two stopped and picked him up, carrying him to the relative safety of some nearby boulders. Seconds after placing Buckley on the ground, Purman was shot through the lower leg, shattering the bones. Not long after, Pipes also suffered a leg wound.

Pipes tried to hobble away but was quickly taken prisoner by the advancing Rebels. Purman would lie on the battlefield all night, surrounded by the screams and moans of wounded and dying men. Many would not survive.

Early the next morning, the fighting resumed, and Purman was struck in his other leg. Spying a nearby lieutenant from Georgia, he cried out for the man to give him some water. The Georgian not only offered Purman his canteen, but he also carried him into a shady area, cleaned his wounds and cut the boots from his swollen feet, bringing Purman some instant relief. As the man prepared to leave, Purman thanked him and gave him his watch as a show of appreciation. Stretcher bearers soon arrived and carried Purman to a nearby field hospital, where surgeons amputated the leg that had been first wounded. He was discharged on a surgeon's certificate on May 20, 1864.

The same day Purman received the Georgian's help, Union troops freed Pipes. Taken to a field hospital, Pipes was transferred to a general hospital in Philadelphia, where he spent the next several months. He returned to the regiment and was leading the company in an effort to stop a Confederate flanking movement at Reams Station, Virginia, in June 1864 when a bullet shattered his right arm. After an agonizing ten-mile ambulance ride over war-torn dirt roads, the arm was amputated the next day at City Station, Virginia. Pipes was hospitalized for several more months before being discharged on a surgeon's certificate on February 17, 1864.

In 1878, Pipes moved to Washington, where he held several staff positions in the War Department, the pension office and the U.S. Senate. He retired in 1920.

Purman returned to Waynesburg College and earned his degree. After graduation, he married Mary Witherow, the daughter of the family he lived with while recuperating from his wounds. He went on to become principal of a private school near Waynesburg. At the same time, he began studying law and eventually opened a private practice. He later moved to Washington and became a medical doctor before taking a position at the U.S. Patent Office.

In 1907, he learned the name of the Georgian who had assisted him at Gettysburg, and he was able to track him down. He invited the man, Thomas Oliver, to come to Washington, where he introduced him to President Theodore Roosevelt. Purman and Oliver exchanged letters for several years.

On October 30, 1896, Purman received the Medal of Honor for his actions in rescuing Private Buckley with Pipes. His citation read:

> *Voluntarily assisted a wounded comrade to a place of apparent safety while the enemy were in close proximity; he received the fire of the enemy and a wound which resulted in the amputation of his left leg. His Medal is in the possession of the Gettysburg Museum and Visitor Center.*

Two years later, on April 5, 1898, Pipes received a Medal of Honor of his own, for actions at both Gettysburg and Reams Station. His citation was more elaborate, saying:

> *While a sergeant and retiring with his company before the rapid advance of the enemy at Gettysburg, he and a companion stopped and carried to a place of safety a wounded and helpless comrade; in this act both he and his companion were severely wounded. A year later, at Reams Station, Va., while commanding a skirmish line, voluntarily assisted in checking a flank movement of the enemy, and while so doing was severely wounded, suffering the loss of an arm.*

Purman died on May 10, 1915, in Washington. Pipes also died in Washington on December 1, 1928. Both men are buried at Arlington National Cemetery, Purman in Section 1 and his friend Pipes not far away, in Section 3.

JAMES PARKE POSTLES, CAPTAIN, COMPANY A, 1ST DELAWARE INFANTRY

On July 2, 1863, the 1st Delaware Infantry was positioned between Taneytown Road and Emmitsburg Road, along what today is Hancock Avenue. Several hundred yards in front of it, in the direction of Seminary Ridge, sat the Bliss farm.

Early in the evening, Confederate sharpshooters gained possession of the farm's barn after a day of fighting to gain the position. Using the barn as a base of operations, the sharpshooters were causing significant problems for the Union line. Members of the 1st Delaware and 12th New Jersey gained control of the house, which sat about sixty yards from the barn. Despite their proximity, the Federals were unable to dislodge the Rebel sharpshooters, who continued to fire into the Federal ranks with great success.

A frustrated General Alexander Hays, division commander, finally sent an order to the 1st Delaware's Colonel Thomas Alfred Smyth to have his troops take the barn and hold it at all hazards. Smyth turned to his men and repeated his instructions, asking who would be willing to carry the order to their men in the house.

Sitting on a nearby rock, Captain James Parke Postles of Company A heard the request. Holding his head in his hands, Postles waited for someone to take the challenge. Postles had been sick for several days and just wanted to sit

James Parke Postles. *Congressional Medal of Honor Society, Mount Pleasant, South Carolina.*

still for a while. However, hearing no one answer, he rose to his feet and said, "I will take it, sir."

Postles was born in Camden, Delaware, on September 28, 1840, and was one of the first to answer his state's call for volunteers when the Civil War began. He first signed up for a three-month enlistment, and when his enlistment was up, he mustered out as a first sergeant. When the regiment reorganized as a three-year regiment, he reenlisted, seeing his first action at Antietam. There, Company A lost nearly half its men, including its captain. Having exemplified himself in the battle, his commanding officer named him the new captain.

Postles mounted his horse and began the trek toward the Bliss farm, crossing the Emmitsburg Road and spurring his horse to a gallop. He immediately regretted his action, as the jarring of the horse in full gallop did nothing to settle his ailing stomach or ease the pounding in his head. Focusing his attention on the farmhouse, he realized that the sharpshooters in the barn had seen him and were now concentrating their fire in his direction.

As he drew closer, the firing became more intense. Postles figured that he was as safe as he could possibly be under the circumstances as long as he remained moving, although he began to wonder what would happen when he stopped to deliver his message. The bullets were coming from every window in the barn, and he reflexively dug his spurs into the flanks of his horse with more than the normal force. The horse responded by rearing and bucking at the discomfort, and Postles said later that he held on to the reins tightly but did nothing to discourage his mount's actions, reasoning that it made him an even harder target for the sharpshooters to hit.

Reaching the house, he shouted out his orders without stopping, slowing only long enough to get an acknowledgement that his message had been received and understood. Once he heard the reply, he immediately turned his horse around and began the return race back to his lines, again drawing heavy fire. Reaching a point where he thought he was finally safe, he slowed his horse, turned and waved his cap in the direction of the Rebels in a show of defiance. His action precipitated an unexpected response, not of bullets, but of a rain of jeers from those in the barn.

The jeers of the Rebels turned to cheers from his company when he reached the Union line, and he was surprised to receive the congratulations of Second Corps commander General Winfield Scott Hancock himself, who had witnessed the incident. His friends all expressed their amazement that neither he nor his horse had been hit.

Back at the Bliss farm, the Union troops launched an attack and took possession of the barn, along with forty Confederate prisoners. To prevent any further problems emanating from the farm, both the house and barn were burned to the ground by the 14th Connecticut Infantry. As the prisoners were brought in, several of them recognized Postles as the horseman they had vainly tried to shoot, with one of them telling Postles that he had personally fired three clean shots at him and missed and that he "reckoned the Yankee's time ain't come yet."

When the war ended, Postles returned to Delaware and worked at his father's leather business. On July 2, 1892, he received word that his daring ride in 1863 had earned him the Medal of Honor. His citation, while recognizing the feat, did not fully describe what he had done. It simply said:

> *Voluntarily delivered an order in the face of heavy fire from the enemy.*

On May 27, 1908, while attending an event at the Wilmington Masonic Temple, he fell down a flight of stairs and suffered a fatal brain injury. His burial took place at the Wilmington and Brandywine Cemetery in Wilmington, Delaware.

Daniel Sickles, Major General, Third Corps

One of the great characters of the Civil War, General Daniel Sickles left a trail of unpaid bills, broken romances and political scandals everywhere he went. Born in New York City, he attended the University of the City of New York, today's New York University. He studied law in the office of Benjamin Butler and was admitted to the bar in 1846. Sickles opened his own law practice and joined the infamous political machine that controlled New York City's political scene, Tammany Hall.

Over the next several years, he served as corporate counsel for New York City, secretary of the United States legation in London and as a member of the New York State Senate. Along the way, he was instrumental in obtaining the land that would become New York's Central Park and received a commission in the 12th New York Militia.

Daniel Edgar Sickles. *Congressional Medal of Honor Society, Mount Pleasant, South Carolina.*

In 1852, at the age of thirty-two, he married his pregnant girlfriend, fifteen-year-old Teresa Bagioli, the daughter of a close friend. Both would have several paramours, leading to what could only be described as a rocky marriage.

In 1855, he was elected to the New York State Senate and to the United States House of Representatives in 1856 and 1858. Although he was only in the state senate for a year, Sickles had sufficient time to be censured by the New York State Assembly for bringing a prostitute onto the Senate floor. He later took the same woman with him on a trip to England, where he presented her to Queen Victoria under the surname of a political opponent.

He would gain a new level of infamy in 1859 when a friend tipped him off anonymously that his wife was having an affair with Philip Barton Key, son of Francis Scott Key, composer of our national anthem. The younger Key was actually a family friend who escorted Teresa to various Washington functions when Sickles was not available. If Sickles really didn't know about the affair, he may have been one of the few people in Washington who didn't. Claiming to be grief-stricken over Teresa's dalliance with Key, he insisted that she confess to the deed in writing. When she did, she refused to use her married name as her signature, using her maiden name instead.

It was only a few days later that Sickles spied Key outside Sickles's home in Washington. Grabbing a gun, he ran outside and chased Key to Lafayette Park, across the street from the White House. Sickles's first shot struck Key in the groin. It has never been established if that was intentional or just a coincidence, but the wound was not fatal. As Key begged for his life, Sickles shot a second time, this time striking him in the chest and killing him. Sickles then walked to the nearby attorney general's office and turned himself in.

Sickles hired Edwin Stanton, who would eventually become President Abraham Lincoln's secretary of war, as his attorney. When the case came to trial, Sickles played the role of the deceived spouse, saying that he couldn't understand how his wife could betray him in such a way. Conveniently ignoring his own illicit relationships, he said he had forgiven her. He then pled temporary insanity, the first time such a defense was ever used in an American courtroom.

Stanton emphasized the portrayal of Sickles as the real victim in the case, stressing how a family friend had seduced his wife. He told the jury that Sickles was a good man but that he was out of his mind with grief when he learned that his wife had not been faithful. His arguments were convincing, and a verdict of not guilty was rendered.

When the Civil War broke out, Sickles saw his opportunity to salvage his honor. He knew that war heroes were held in the highest esteem, and he convinced New York's Governor Edwin Morgan to allow him to raise a company of volunteer troops. Once that was done, he sought and received approval to organize an entire brigade. The result was the 70th, 71st, 72nd, 73rd and 74th New York Infantries, which would collectively become known as the Excelsior Brigade. Drawing on his political connections and his prior militia experience, he became colonel of the 70th New York. In September 1861 he was promoted to brigadier general of volunteers, once again a political appointment.

Unable or unwilling to change his character, he gained as many political enemies as he did political friends, and he was forced to relinquish his command in March 1862 when Congress refused to confirm his commission. Once again calling in political favors, he reclaimed his rank two months later when the Senate confirmed him by a 19–18 vote.

On January 16, 1863, President Abraham Lincoln nominated Sickles for promotion to major general. The promotion was confirmed by the U.S. Senate on March 9, followed by the official appointment by the president two days later. The timing wasn't important to Sickles, however. He had already been given command of the Third Corps by his good friend and fellow womanizer, Major General Joseph Hooker, in February. The appointment was in keeping with Sickles's controversial nature, as it made him the only corps commander without a West Point education.

At Gettysburg, he was ordered by Major General George Meade to have his corps take a defensive position on July 2, 1863, along the southern portion of Cemetery Ridge, anchoring his northern end to the Second Corps and his southern end at Little Round Top. Once there, Sickles saw the Peach Orchard in his front; believing its slightly higher elevation gave him an advantage, he moved his men without orders to that location. This stretched his corps too thin and created a salient that the Confederates were able to exploit. It also infuriated Meade, who rushed to speak with

Sickles but got there too late. With the Confederates already attacking as part of Lieutenant General James Longstreet's Assault, there was no time to reposition the Third Corps.

Longstreet's troops routed Sickles's Third Corps, decimating it. In the attack, Sickles was wounded in the leg by a cannonball at the Peter Trostle farm. A monument stands today at the site of his wounding. Hiding the pain of his mangled limb as he was being carried off the field on a stretcher, he famously drew himself up on one elbow and made a show of casually puffing on a cigar to rally his men. The leg was later amputated, and Sickles had the amputated limb sent in a coffin-shaped box to the Army Medical Museum (now the National Museum of Health and Medicine) in Washington, D.C. For a time, the bones were used as a teaching aid about battlefield trauma, and Sickles often visited the exhibit of his shattered bones. The display has since been upgraded, with the bones and a cannonball similar to one that caused his wound placed together in a plastic case.

Sickles remained in the army until the war's end, receiving appointments as brevet brigadier general and major general. He spent years after the war attacking Meade's character and defending his decision to move to the Peach Orchard. He also wrote numerous anonymous newspaper articles that declared him the reason the Union won the battle at Gettysburg. Historians still debate the pros and cons of his move.

To his credit, however, he was active in Reconstruction and vigorously pursued fair treatment for freed slaves. He received an appointment as colonel of the 42nd United States Infantry (Veteran Reserve Corps) and retired as a major general. Over the next several years, he served as U.S. minister to Spain (where in typical Sickles fashion he had an affair with Queen Isabella II), chairman of the New York State Civil Service Commission, sheriff of New York County and on the Gettysburg Battlefield Memorial Commission, among other positions.

As chairman of the New York State Monument Commission, he obtained funding for the Excelsior Brigade monument on the Gettysburg battlefield. The monument was to have a bust of Sickles in its center. However, that never materialized because there was insufficient money left when time came to commission the bust. The reason for the cash shortage? An audit revealed that some $28,000 had been embezzled from the fund, and all indications were that Sickles was responsible, although it was never proven.

In 1892, he was elected to Congress once again, serving from 1893 to 1895, and was instrumental in the development of Gettysburg National Military Park. When asked why he never had a statue to himself at Gettysburg, he would ignore the cash shortage for the Excelsior Brigade monument bust and proclaim that the entire battlefield was his monument.

On October 30, 1897, Sickles was awarded the Medal of Honor for

> *most conspicuous gallantry on the field vigorously contesting the advance of the enemy and continuing to encourage his troops after being himself severely wounded.*

Sickles died of a cerebral hemorrhage on May 3, 1914, at the age of ninety-four and was buried at Arlington National Cemetery.

Note: This section was adapted from one that originally appeared on the website of the Congressional Medal of Honor Society.

John Lonergan, Captain, Company A, 13th Vermont Infantry

John Lonergan was born on April 7, 1837, in Carrick-on-Suir, County Donegal, Ireland. He and his family immigrated to the United States in 1848, where he became a leader of the Fenian Brotherhood, an organization committed to self-rule and obtaining independence from Britain. The family settled in Vermont, where young John worked alongside his father as a cooper.

In 1862, he and a group of his friends formed a company of Vermonters of Irish descent. His plan was twofold: help the Union army in its battle with the Confederacy but also, perhaps more importantly in the long run, burnish his military skills, which would be useful in attaining freedom for Ireland. The group they formed was known as the Emmett Guards of Burlington and eventually become Company A of the 13th Vermont Infantry.

In October 1862, the regiment set up camp on East Capitol Hill in Washington and within two weeks had suffered its first two deaths: Private Isaac N. Brooks, age sixteen, of Company E and Lieutenant Nathaniel Jones of Company B, both of typhoid fever.

On the afternoon of July 2, 1863, the regiment set up on Cemetery Ridge, forming the right of Union General George Stannard's Brigade. It had arrived the previous evening after a week of long marches, averaging eighteen miles per day. The troops reported to the 3rd Division of the First Corps, which had suffered serious losses on the first day of fighting at Gettysburg.

When Battery C of the 5th United States Artillery was in danger of being overrun and captured, General Winfield Scott Hancock sent orders for

John Lonergan. *Congressional Medal of Honor Society, Mount Pleasant, South Carolina.*

the regiment to respond in support. The Vermonters moved forward and were able to save the four guns, capturing two additional Confederate guns in the process along the Emmitsburg Road. Lonergan and Company A were instrumental in this action.

While still in that area, the regiment came under fire from a nearby house owned by Peter and Susan Rodgers. Lonergan took his company and surrounded the house while still under fire. Shouting over the din of the battle, Lonergan ordered those inside the house to surrender. The Alabamans who had been shooting at Lonergan and Company A discussed their options and then decided to lay down their weapons and come out. When they did, Lonergan and his men were surprised to see that they had captured eighty-one prisoners.

Gettysburg would prove to be Lonergan's last battle. The 13th Vermont participated in the defense against Pickett's Charge the next day and then joined in the pursuit of Lee's army following the battle. On July 8, it was ordered home. Lonergan and the rest of the 13th Vermont mustered out on July 21, 1863.

Following his service, Lonergan helped organize two raids into Canada from St. Albans, Vermont, hoping to pressure Britain, which was ruling Canada as a colony at the time, into surrendering control of Ireland. Both raids ended in failure.

On October 28, 1893, the young Irishman who wanted to learn military tactics that would aid in getting Britain to relinquish control over Ireland was awarded the Medal of Honor for his actions at Gettysburg. His citation says:

> *Gallantry in the recapture of four guns and the capture of two additional guns from the enemy; also the capture of a number of prisoners.*

Lonergan died in Montreal on August 6, 1902. He was buried at St. Joseph's Cemetery in Burlington, Vermont.

On May 8, 2010, nearly 147 years after Lonergan performed so heroically at Gettysburg, his hometown in Ireland, Carrick-on-Suir, dedicated a memorial to her native son. In 2013, his adopted home, Burlington, Vermont, did the same.

George Washington Roosevelt, First Sergeant, Company K, 26th Pennsylvania Infantry

George Washington Roosevelt was born in Chester County, Pennsylvania, on February 14, 1844, the fourth son of James Solomon and Esther (Vickery) Roosevelt. Little is known about the Roosevelt family or George's early years, but it is known that he enlisted in Company K of the 26th Pennsylvania on May 31, 1861, as a corporal.

The regiment spent its first five months in the defense of Washington, D.C. It then moved around through Maryland and Virginia until participating in the Siege of Yorktown in April and May 1862. From there, it got relatively active, fighting at the Battle of Williamsburg, Battle of Seven Pines, Oak Grove, Savage's Station, White Oak Swamp, Glendale and Malvern Hill, all in the space of less than two months. After a brief respite of six weeks, another series of skirmishes in August brought it to Manassas, Virginia, where the first battle of any size had launched the Civil War on July 21, 1861.

It was now August 30, 1862, and Manassas was about to see its second battle. On this date, nineteen-year-old George was first called a hero for recapturing the regimental colors after they had been captured by the Confederates. The Union army suffered a defeat on that battlefield, and the regiment reflected that loss, losing two officers killed and sixty-three men killed or wounded. The regimental flag was captured by the Rebels, and in brutal hand-to-hand combat, George recovered the colors, to high praise from his superior officers. He received a promotion to sergeant as a reward.

Almost one year later, on July 3, 1863, George showed uncommon valor once again. Now a first sergeant, he lined up along Emmitsburg Road with the regiment. The regiment then launched an attack and penetrated the Confederate line. Through the smoke, George could make out the figure of someone holding a flag aloft. From the direction the man was facing, George knew that it had to be a Rebel flag bearer. Getting closer, he could make out the colors, confirming his suspicion. The man was facing slightly away from George and was not aware of his presence.

Choosing to capture the color bearer rather than shoot him, George rushed toward the man and spun him around. Holding his gun on the startled Southerner, he demanded his surrender, including his flag. Clutching the captured banner, he began to march his prisoner back to the Union line. Before he reached his destination, however, he was struck in the leg

George Washington Roosevelt. *Congressional Medal of Honor Society, Mount Pleasant, South Carolina.*

by a bullet, knocking him down. His prisoner, seeing his opportunity, escaped as George writhed in pain, still clenching the captured colors. When the fighting subsided, George was carried to a field hospital, where his leg was deemed to be so badly mangled that the only viable treatment was amputation. He would never fight again and was eventually discharged on a surgeon's certificate in March 1864 after being awarded a brevet promotion to captain.

George Roosevelt recovered from his wound and entered into a thirty-year career as a diplomat, serving in Sydney, Auckland, Saint Helena, Matanzas, Bordeaux and Brussels from 1877 to 1907. Along the way, however, his grateful nation presented him with a Medal of Honor for his actions at Bull Run and Gettysburg. The Medal was presented to him on July 2, 1897, the thirty-fourth anniversary of his heroism at Gettysburg. The accompanying citation read:

> *At Bull Run, Va., recaptured the colors, which had been seized by the enemy. At Gettysburg captured a Confederate color bearer and colors, in which effort he was severely wounded.*

Roosevelt died on April 15, 1907, in Brussels, Belgium, and was returned to the United States for burial at Oak Hill Cemetery in Washington, D.C.

His story did not end with his burial, however. In May 2003, his Medal was illegally put up for auction on eBay with another Medal of Honor, that of Seaman Robert Blume, who had earned his Medal in the Spanish-American War. The Federal Bureau of Investigation was alerted to the sale, and an undercover agent made the purchase from a husband and wife from Mississauga, Ontario. With the assistance of Canadian authorities, the two were arrested in Buffalo immediately after the sale was transacted.

Unable to locate families for the two men, the Medals were donated to the Congressional Medal of Honor Society in Mount Pleasant, South Carolina.

Part V

THE THIRD DAY OF BATTLE, JULY 3, 1863

Hugh Carey, Sergeant, Company E, 82nd New York Infantry

Hugh Carey was born in Ireland in 1841. After immigrating to the United States, he settled in New York City, from where he enlisted in the 82nd New York Infantry as a corporal in Company E on April 18, 1861, at age twenty. His service records indicate that he was promoted to sergeant on an unknown date, sometime prior to the Battle of Gettysburg. He was one of three men named Carey in the 82nd New York. They are not believed to be related.

When the regiment arrived at Gettysburg, it was placed on picket duty with the 15th Massachusetts Volunteers. The commander of the regiment was Lieutenant Colonel James Huston, also born in Ireland. He was killed on the first day of fighting, with command of the regiment falling to Captain John Darrow. As a harbinger of Carey's action on July 3, the regiment captured the flag of the 48th Georgia Infantry.

On July 3, the final day of the battle, the 82nd New York moved to a position not far from the Copse of Trees on Cemetery Ridge. From that position, it watched nervously as the gray line of Southern troops advanced from Seminary Ridge, across Emmitsburg Road and toward its position. It had just endured the Confederate artillery bombardment that preceded the infantry's advance, and Carey was trying to calm the troops under his charge. It wasn't easy; he was trying to calm himself at the same time.

The sun that had been shining brightly before the bombardment was now hidden by the smoke of battle, bathing the field in an eerie glow. The

Hugh Carey captured a Confederate flag in the field seen behind this photo of the regimental monument. *Author photo.*

advancing men coming directly toward them now were Major General James L. Kemper's, although they were just Rebels to Carey and the rest of Company E. Tattered flags waved at the front of the line, each one proudly showing the effects of previous battles. Soon, entire gaps appeared in the line when the Union artillery found its mark. But still they came. As much as

Carey hated the Confederacy for trying to split the Union, he admired the bravery of the men he was facing.

Then the order came to fire as the line came within range. Carey was relieved that now he and the rest of the regiment could do something other than wait. The crack of muskets came from both sides now, and bodies littered both sides of the stone wall that marked the Union line. Reaching a point where they thought they could breach the wall, the Rebels broke into a run, unleashing that fearful yell that Carey had come to expect when the lines drew closer.

The Federal line rose to meet the charge, and the fighting became hand to hand. Bayonets were used, muskets were turned and used as clubs, those who had their weapons already loaded fired their charges directly into the faces of the men in front of them and oaths and curses rang out. Both sides fought desperately, knowing that the outcome of this charge would determine the battle's victor.

Carey, now wounded, lunged for the flag carried by the color bearer from the 7th Virginia. For just a few seconds, the two struggled to get control, Carey intent on capturing it and the Virginian just as determined to maintain possession. Then, with one final tug, Carey ripped the flag from its staff. The flag bearer tried to strike Carey with the staff but missed, and seeing the rest of the Confederate line falling back, he reluctantly joined in the retreat. As Carey watched, a shot struck him, knocking him to the ground.

Catching his breath, Carey rose to his feet and began slowly making his way to the rear, still carrying his prize. He later learned that someone else had also captured a flag, that one from the 1st Virginia Infantry, giving the regiment three captured flags at Gettysburg.

After recuperating from his wounds, Carey remained with the 82nd New York until his discharge in May 1864. On February 6, 1888, he was rewarded for his effort at Gettysburg with the presentation of the Medal of Honor, his citation reading:

> *Captured the flag of the 7th Virginia Infantry (C.S.A.), being twice wounded in the effort.*

Carey never knew that he had received the Medal. Two years earlier, on March 26, 1886, he died in Brooklyn at the age of forty-five. He rests at Brooklyn's Holy Cross Cemetery.

Frederick Fuger, First Sergeant, Battery A, 4th United States Light Artillery

Born in Germany on June 18, 1836, eighteen-year-old Frederick Fuger was determined to come to the United States. He traveled to France, boarded a ship and landed in New York on April 3, 1854. He immediately fell in love with his new home.

In August 1856, before the rumbles of several states seceding from the Union became reality, Fuger joined the 4th United States Light Artillery. His five-year enlistment was just ending when Fort Sumter was fired on. Although not a citizen, Frederick decided to reenlist to fight the Rebellion. His reenlistment got him promoted to first sergeant.

The battery arrived in Gettysburg on the second day of the battle, July 2, 1863, and set up its guns with Brigadier General Alexander Stewart Webb's Second Division, Second Corps. Almost immediately, the men were pressed into service in an artillery engagement. Their participation extended throughout the rest of the day. On July 3, they were at the Angle, not knowing that their location would be the focal point of Pickett's Charge. Most of the morning was relatively quiet, at least when it was compared to what was to come. Around noon, the Confederate artillery opened the fighting with a deafening salvo from nearly 150 cannons. Many of the shells overshot their target, but enough found their mark that Battery A was ripped to pieces. Only one workable gun remained of the original six. When the artillery finished their deadly work, the Confederate infantry advanced.

Battery A fired repeatedly as the onslaught continued. Casualties rapidly mounted until the entire battery crew consisted only of Fuger; his commander, First Lieutenant Alonzo Cushing; and a few gunners, most of them already wounded. Among the wounded was Cushing, whose story appears later in this part. Feeling the effects of his wounds, Cushing could barely stand, but he refused to retreat. Fuger propped Cushing up so he could give commands to the remaining gun crew. As the Rebel line drew nearer, the battery stepped up its pace, the gunners working feverishly. Then Cushing was killed, and command devolved to Fuger. As several Southerners broke through the Union line, he ordered his men to fight as infantry.

Frederick Fuger. *Congressional Medal of Honor Society, Mount Pleasant, South Carolina.*

The battle was now hand to hand. Then, slowly, the Confederate attack stalled, and they began their retreat, to the cheers of the Union troops. In the fighting, the battery had lost forty-five of its ninety-three men either killed or wounded and eighty-three of its ninety horses killed.

Fuger was promoted to second lieutenant later in 1863 and commanded Battery A through the end of the war. At war's end, he remained in the army until his retirement in 1900 with the rank of major. Over the course of the Civil War, Fuger fought in sixty-three engagements and battles and was wounded twice. In 1904, an act of Congress promoted him to lieutenant colonel. Despite this envious record, his proudest achievement came in 1888, when he became an American citizen.

On August 24, 1897, he received the Medal of Honor, with his citation reading:

> *All the officers of his battery having been killed or wounded and five of its guns disabled in Pickett's assault, he succeeded to the command and fought the remaining gun with most distinguished gallantry until the battery was ordered withdrawn.*

Frederick Fuger passed away on October 13, 1913, in Washington and was buried at Arlington National Cemetery.

CHRISTOPHER FLYNN, CORPORAL, COMPANY K, 14TH CONNECTICUT INFANTRY

ELIJAH WILLIAM BACON, PRIVATE, COMPANY K, 14TH CONNECTICUT INFANTRY

WILLIAM B. HINCKS, SERGEANT MAJOR, 14TH CONNECTICUT INFANTRY

The 14th Connecticut Infantry experienced the rare situation in which three of its members captured flags, not only in the same battle but also in the same action in that battle. Corporal Christopher Flynn and Private Elijah William Bacon of Company K each captured a flag, while Sergeant Major William B. Hincks of the regiment did the same. All three flags were captured on the third day of the battle while the regiment was defending along Cemetery Ridge.

Flynn was born in Ireland in December 1828. It is not known when he came to the United States, but he was known to have settled in Sprague, Connecticut. Regimental records show that he enlisted with the 14th Connecticut in August 1862 at the age of thirty-three, making him much older than most of those in the regiment. He would survive the war despite suffering a serious wound at Laurel Hill, Virginia.

William B. Hincks. *Congressional Medal of Honor Society, Mount Pleasant, South Carolina.*

Bacon was born in Burlington, Connecticut, in 1836 and is believed to have mustered in at the same time as Flynn. A stone carver in civilian life, he married Angeline Shelly just before enlisting. He was court-martialed six weeks before arriving at Gettysburg for refusing to arrest some men who had been disturbing the peace. He was fined fourteen dollars, one dollar more than what he earned as a soldier in a month. On May 6, 1864, less than a year after Gettysburg, he was killed at the Battle of the Wilderness.

Hincks was the youngest of the three, having been born in Bucksport, Maine, in 1841. He moved to Bridgeport, Connecticut, as a young boy and dropped out of school to enlist. His enlistment also came in August 1862.

The regiment was assigned to picket duty on July 1, some two miles from the fighting. It was not until the evening of July 1, 1863, that it arrived at the battlefield, after most of the first day's fighting had ended. Commanded by Major Theodore G. Ellis, the men formed into position along what is present-day Hancock Avenue on Cemetery Ridge and remained in the same general location until the end of the battle. The regiment was instrumental in the capture and burning of the Bliss farm on July 3, an action described in Part IV.

Later that same day, the regiment was part of the Union battle line that endured the artillery bombardment prior to Pickett's Charge. Before the artillery began firing, most of the troops rested, ate or just relaxed. Only the ambulances and surgeons were busy, either treating the wounded from the day before or preparing for the wounded that were sure to come in the next few hours. Once the barrage began, most of the men stopped what they were doing and began to pray. Many of those carrying playing cards or dice tossed them away, not wishing to die with the devil's instruments in their pockets.

14th Connecticut Infantry monument. Flynn, Bacon and Hincks all captured Confederate flags during Pickett's Charge in the area behind the regimental monument. *Author photo.*

As the barrage ended, Captain William Arnold's 1st Rhode Island Light Artillery, which the 14th Connecticut had been supporting, pulled back, badly damaged. This required the Nutmeg Staters to fill the vacated gap, spreading themselves out until they were in one single line.

Then came the Confederate infantry. The New Englanders peered anxiously over the top of the stone wall in their front as the gray line advanced. Wounded men and horses screamed out in agony, adding to the cacophony. Sweat poured off each man, partly from the intense heat and partly from anxiety. Many dumped the contents of their cartridge boxes onto the ground to speed up their loading.

Rebel pickets fell into the line as it passed, and Union pickets slowly withdrew, some of them stopping occasionally to fire at the oncoming line. Each man behind the wall resisted the urge to shoot, remembering their orders from General Alexander Hays that no gun should be fired until the Rebels reached Emmitsburg Road. When the order came, each man fired simultaneously in what sounded like one loud shot. Gaps in the Confederate line opened as men fell. But still they came, their blue-clad opponents in awe of what they were seeing.

As the line drew closer, the 14th Connecticut and several other regiments could be contained no longer. Jumping over the wall, they met the advancing line. What had started with the horrendous artillery duel had now eroded into hand-to-hand combat, the most primitive way to fight.

Less than fifty yards in front, a flag bearer had placed his regimental colors. The flag bearer was lying on the ground to avoid the horrendous onslaught of bullets but was still holding his flag erect. Several others were also lying in the immediate area, afraid to stand and appearing confused as to whether they should advance or retreat. Spying the flag, Major Ellis called for volunteers to capture it. Immediately, Hincks rushed forward, along with Lieutenant George Bingham and Major J.C. Broach. Bingham was shot down almost as soon as he began running. Hincks and Broach dashed forward, Hincks the faster of the two. He grabbed the flag from the startled flag bearer and raced back with Broach right behind. Shots sped past them, but both reached the wall unscathed. There, Hincks examined his booty, seeing that it belonged to the 14th Tennessee Infantry. The banner contained the names of twelve battles where the regiment had fought.

When the Confederate line eventually began to withdraw, the Connecticut men began to follow, bringing in those who wished to surrender. Flynn spied the flag of the 52nd North Carolina and raced ahead to knock down the flag bearer and snatch the flag belonging to the 52nd North Carolina. In much the same fashion, Bacon captured the flag of the 16th North Carolina Infantry.

After the war, Hincks became a bank executive and helped P.T. Barnum found the Barnum Museum and the Bridgeport Hospital. In 1866, he married Mary Louise Hart. Flynn returned to Connecticut and lived a quiet life, supporting himself by working at various odd jobs. It is not known if he married, nor is there much information of any kind about his civilian life.

On December 6, 1864, all three—Flynn, Bacon and Hincks—were awarded the Medal of Honor for capturing the flags. Bacon's award was presented posthumously. Flynn's and Bacon's citations were worded nearly identically, with Flynn's reading:

> *Capture of flag of 52nd North Carolina Infantry (C.S.A.)*

Bacon's read:

> *Capture of flag of the 16th North Carolina regiment (C.S.A.).*

Hincks's was much more detailed:

> *During the highwater mark of Pickett's Charge on 3 July 1863 the colors of the 14th Tennessee Infantry C.S.A. were planted 50 yards in front of the center of Sgt. Maj. Hincks' regiment. There were no Confederates standing near it but several were lying down around it. Upon a call for volunteers by Maj. Ellis, commanding, to capture this flag, this soldier and two others leaped the wall. One companion was instantly shot. Sgt. Maj. Hincks outran his remaining companion, running straight and swift for the colors amid a storm of shot. Swinging his saber over the prostrate Confederates and uttering a terrific yell, he seized the flag and hastily returned to his lines. The 14th Tenn. carried 12 battle honors on its flag. The devotion to duty shown by Sgt. Maj. Hincks gave encouragement to many of his comrades at a crucial moment of the battle.*

All three Medals were presented by Major General George Meade at a review of the 2nd Army Corps headquarters at Peebles's House near Petersburg, Virginia.

Flynn died in Sprague, Connecticut, on October 15, 1889, and was interred at St. Mary's Cemetery in Baltic, Connecticut. Hincks died on

November 7, 1903, in Bridgeport, Connecticut, and was buried at that city's Mountain Grove Cemetery. Bacon's remains were returned to Berlin, Connecticut, and buried at Maple Grove Cemetery.

Henry D. O'Brien, Corporal, Company E, 1st Minnesota Infantry

A reader would be hard-pressed to find a more legendary regiment than the 1st Minnesota Infantry at Gettysburg. And to find someone who survived from that regiment would be even more difficult. Henry D. O'Brien not only survived, but he also performed with such heroism that he would be awarded the Medal of Honor.

Henry was born in Calais, Maine, on the frigid morning of January 21, 1842. When he was fifteen years old, the family moved to Saint Anthony Falls, Minnesota. On August 13, 1861, he enlisted in the 1st Minnesota Infantry, Company E.

Every state represented in the Civil War has a regiment with "1st" in its name. However, the 1st Minnesota was the only one that could say it was truly the real "first," having been the first group of volunteers to respond to the attack on Fort Sumter. Minnesota Governor Alexander Ramsey was in Washington when word came of the firing on the fort. He immediately offered one thousand men to President Lincoln, an offer the president accepted. While Henry was not one of the first group to sign up, he was proud to be a part of the regiment that was.

The regiment, under the command of Colonel William Colvill, became legendary on July 2, 1863, at Gettysburg. That afternoon, General Daniel Sickles had moved his Third Corps forward to what he believed to be a more advantageous position in the Peach Orchard. That action is described in Part IV. When the Third Corps was driven back, two Confederate brigades pursued. If the Confederates breached the gap that had been created when Sickles moved his troops forward, the Union army could be devastated.

The 1st Minnesota was already shorthanded. Company C was detached on provost duty at division headquarters, Company L was attached to the 1st U.S. Sharpshooters, Company F was held in reserve and 20 men were assigned to the division hospital. Only 262 men and officers were on hand when General Winfield Scott Hancock saw them as his only option to hold the advancing Rebels until reinforcements arrived. He ordered them to do

Henry D. O'Brien. *Congressional Medal of Honor Society, Mount Pleasant, South Carolina.*

just that. Despite recognizing the assignment as suicidal, the regiment responded with a bayonet charge.

Outnumbered by an estimated six to one, O'Brien and the rest of the 1st Minnesota plunged into the Rebel line. The regiment's flag fell five times. It was picked up each time. By the time they reached the oncoming Southerners, the regiment had been spread out so much that the men found themselves fighting alone or, at best, with only a few of their comrades. As would be expected, the regiment was decimated, but it accomplished its objective. The Confederates advanced no farther. General Hancock later said of the regiment, "No soldiers on any field, in this or any other country, ever displayed grander heroism."

Historians believe that the 1st Minnesota saved the Union army that day. Recognizing the importance of what the regiment had accomplished, President Calvin Coolidge would remark some sixty years later, "Colonel Colvill and those eight companies of the First Minnesota are entitled to rank as the saviors of their country."

Of the 262 who began the charge, only 47 Minnesotans emerged from the fight. The 82 percent casualty rate is believed to be the largest by any United States regiment in a single day of battle. Henry O'Brien was one of the 47 survivors. That evening, his officers were calling him a hero among a regiment of heroes. Under heavy fire, he had stopped to pick up a badly wounded Private Ernest Jefferson and carry him to safety behind the Union line. If you've read this far, you know that men have been awarded the Medal of Honor for that very deed. But Henry O'Brien was not finished.

In Pickett's Charge the next day, O'Brien stepped up once again. As the 28th Virginia Infantry approached the Union line, his regiment attacked its flank. In that action, color bearer Corporal John Dehn was shot down, and the flag's staff was shot into two pieces. O'Brien picked up the section that contained the now tattered flag and led the men into another hand-to hand fight. Momentarily rendered unconscious when he was struck in the head by a spent bullet, he maintained a viselike grip on the banner. Rising up, he continued to advance, receiving a second wound. This wound, to his hand, also failed to stop him, and he was able to bring the flag back to

O'Brien's heroic actions are captured on this bas relief on the regiment's monument. *Author photo.*

the line safely when the Confederates withdrew. O'Brien had an impetuous personality, and veterans of the fight later admitted that they blamed him fleetingly for placing the flag in peril, but then they praised him for bravely keeping the regiment's banner in front of every other flag.

A monument to the regiment along the Union line off Hancock Avenue marks the location from which the July 3 countercharge against the 28th Virginia was made. That monument contains a bronze bas-relief depiction of the action. The figure depicting O'Brien can be plainly seen in the center, carrying the regimental flag.

After the war, O'Brien returned to Minnesota briefly and then moved to St. Louis. Married to Emma Sinclair, he worked there as a government pension agent. On April 9, 1890, he received the Medal of Honor for his actions on July 3, with his citation noting:

> *Taking up the colors where they had fallen, he rushed ahead of his regiment, close to the muzzles of the enemy's guns, and engaged in the desperate struggle in which the enemy was defeated, and though severely wounded, he held the colors until wounded a second time.*

Henry O'Brien died of pneumonia in St. Louis on November 2, 1902, and was interred at Bellefontaine Cemetery there.

JOHN H. ROBINSON, PRIVATE, COMPANY I, 19TH MASSACHUSETTS INFANTRY

JOSEPH H. DECASTRO, CORPORAL, COMPANY I, 19TH MASSACHUSETTS INFANTRY

BENJAMIN H. JELLISON, SERGEANT, COMPANY C, 19TH MASSACHUSETTS INFANTRY

BENJAMIN FRANKLIN FALLS, COLOR SERGEANT, COMPANY A, 19TH MASSACHUSETTS INFANTRY

A large number of the Medals of Honor earned on July 3, 1863, resulted from the capture of flags during Pickett's Charge. The 19th Massachusetts did more than its part by taking four enemy flags. Two of those were taken by members of Company I, Private John H. Robinson and Corporal Joseph H. DeCastro. Sergeant Benjamin Jellison of Company C captured another, as did Color Sergeant Benjamin Franklin Falls of Company A. A fifth member of the regiment, Major Edmund Rice, also earned a Medal of Honor in the same action but for a different reason, and his story is discussed separately.

John H. Robinson was born in Ireland in 1846. Beyond that, little is known about his life until his enlistment in the 19th Massachusetts on August 30, 1861. He was initially assigned to Company H. Either his birth date is incorrect or he lied about his age when he enlisted, which was not that uncommon. The birth date and enlistment date shown would mean that he was fifteen years old. However, his muster information indicates that he was nineteen. Whatever his age, he transferred into Company I on December 1, 1861.

Much more is known about DeCastro, who was born on November 14, 1844, in Boston. His father, Domingo DeCastro, had emigrated from Spain. Joseph was placed in the Worcester State Reform School at some point for being stubborn, a designation for children who were overly defiant. His enlistment was recorded as July 12, 1861, when he was placed in Company F. Discharged in 1865, he reenlisted five years later into the 6th U.S. Cavalry and remained in service until 1874. In civilian life, he was active in the Grand Army of the Republic.

Benjamin Franklin Falls was born on July 1, 1824, in Portsmouth, New Hampshire, and is nearly as anonymous as Robinson. He was the only son out of three children born to Benjamin H. and Mary (Alley) Falls. He enlisted at the age of thirty-six in August 1861 as a private in Company A of

Left: Benjamin Franklin Falls. *Congressional Medal of Honor Society, Mount Pleasant, South Carolina.*

Right: Benjamin H. Jellison. *Congressional Medal of Honor Society, Mount Pleasant, South Carolina.*

the 19th Massachusetts. He reenlisted on December 21, 1863. Little has been found about his personal life.

The last of the four Medal recipients, Benjamin H. Jellison, also lived in relative anonymity. Even his obituary shed little light onto his life. Born in Newburyport, Massachusetts, on December 29, 1845, he enlisted as a private in Company C on July 26, 1861. Jellison was wounded at the Battle of Oak Grove on June 25, 1862, and again on June 3, 1864, at Cold Harbor. He also reenlisted on December 21, 1863. He married Elizabeth (Morrison) Jellison in 1867, and they had three children. Nothing more is known about his life as a civilian.

At Gettysburg, the 19th Massachusetts was commanded by Colonel Arthur F. Devereux. At about 9:00 p.m. on July 1, the regiment reached a point on Taneytown Road about two miles from the battlefield. The next morning, after a quick breakfast, the troops moved into position on Cemetery Ridge, where they spent a relatively uneventful day until about 5:00 p.m.

That was about the time Sickles's Third Corps was being pushed back, and Devereux and 42nd New York commander Colonel James E. Mallon were ordered to support Sickles. The two regiments rushed to assist and, upon reaching the rear of the Third Corps, they asked an officer where they should position themselves and what they were being asked to accomplish.

The officer only said they should assist General Andrew Humphreys's Division. Both colonels protested that two small regiments with only 290 men together would be of little assistance to an entire division when that division was broken and retreating in confusion. The officer made no comment and rode off.

Now left to themselves with no direct orders, the two colonels decided to form up behind a small knoll, wait until the retreating line had passed and then deliver a volley into the pursuing Confederate troops. Upon doing that, the two regiments immediately retreated to avoid capture. In the retreat, Jellison was near the color bearer when he saw the man go down. Jellison picked up the colors to save them from capture and continued with the retreat. The regiment eventually returned to its original position, where the men spent the night. Jellison was promoted to sergeant for saving the flag.

On July 3, the troops from Massachusetts saw little activity until the artillery barrage marking the beginning of Pickett's Charge. Positioned just behind and to the left of the Copse of Trees, they could see the advancing Confederate infantry all too well. The New York Independent Battery, which the regiment was supporting, fell silent, with only the captain, lieutenant and a sergeant left standing. The captain ran to Devereux and asked him to send men to help fire the guns. Jellison was one of those who ran to the battery, but when Devereux spotted him, he ordered Jellison back to carry the colors he had saved a day earlier.

Nearing the Union line, the Confederates broke into a run, many headed directly for the stone wall where the 19th and 20th Massachusetts were positioned. Given the order to countercharge, the men from Massachusetts were soon engaged in a hand-to-hand struggle. In the melee, Jellison and Robinson both spied the Rebel color bearer for the 57th Virginia. Rushing to him, they snatched the flag from the startled man's grasp and ordered him to surrender. The man complied, and Jellison marched him back as a prisoner, along with several others who gave themselves up.

While Jellison was escorting prisoners to the rear, DeCastro added a flag of his own to the regiment's growing collection. Carrying the Massachusetts state flag, he rushed the flag bearer for the 19th Virginia Infantry. Using his own flagstaff as a weapon, he knocked the Virginian to the ground and grabbed his flag. He then took the colors to Devereux and rushed back into the battle. Devereux later said that "a man broke through my lines and thrust a Rebel battle flag into my hands. He never said a word and darted back."

The 19th Massachusetts marker. Robinson, DeCastro, Jellison and Falls each captured Confederate flags in an area about 119 yards south-southeast of the marker. *Author photo.*

The details of Falls's actions are sketchy. He is credited only with capturing an enemy flag from an unknown regiment. However, he was involved in one amusing exchange that was recorded by Captain John G.B. Adams. According to Adams, Falls had just captured his flag and returned to the regiment with it draped over his shoulder. An officer stopped him and told him that he had to turn the flag over so it could be sent to the War Department in Washington. Falls glared at the officer for a few seconds and replied, "Well, there are lots of them over behind the wall. Go and get one; I did."

On December 1, 1864, the four were awarded the Medal of Honor. The citations were all very simple, with DeCastro's saying:

> *Capture of flag of 19th Virginia regiment (C.S.A.).*

He was the first Spanish American citizen to receive the Medal.

Robinson's citation was nearly identical:

> *Capture of flag of 57th Virginia Infantry (C.S.A.)*

Jellison's was only slightly more detailed:

> *Capture of flag of 57th Virginia Infantry (C.S.A.). He also assisted in taking prisoners.*

Falls was killed on May 10, 1864, at the Battle of the Wilderness, and his award was posthumous, saying simply:

> *Capture of flag.*

Obviously, Falls was the first of the four to die. His remains now lay in rest at Pine Grove Cemetery in Lynn, Massachusetts. Next was Robinson, who died at the age of thirty-seven on November 30, 1883. He is buried at St. Benedict Cemetery in West Roxbury, Massachusetts. DeCastro followed next, passing away in New York City on May 8, 1892. He was interred at Newark, New Jersey's Fairmount Cemetery. Last of the four was Jellison, who lived until April 5, 1924. He is buried at Elmwood Cemetery in Haverhill, Massachusetts.

William E. Miller, Captain, Company H, 3rd Pennsylvania Cavalry

It isn't often that a soldier can disobey an order and end up being rewarded, but William E. Miller of the 3rd Pennsylvania Cavalry is one of the few who could say it happened to him.

Miller was born in West Hill, Cumberland County, Pennsylvania, on February 5, 1836, the son of Andrew and Eleanor (Umberger) Miller. When his father became an invalid, William took over as manager of the family farm while still a teenager. Seeking adventure, he enlisted at age sixteen in a local company of horsemen known as the Big Spring Adamantine Guard. He married his childhood sweetheart, Elizabeth Ann Hocker, and they had two daughters, Caroline and Lizzie. His marriage ended tragically when Elizabeth died of typhoid just two years later.

On August 17, 1861, the Adamantine Guard became Company H of the 3rd Pennsylvania Cavalry, and Miller was named a lieutenant based on his nine years of service with the Guard. He became a captain after the Battle of Antietam as a reward for his gallantry in that battle. In March 1862, while still mourning Elizabeth's death, he received word from her mother that Lizzie had also died.

The 3rd Pennsylvania Cavalry was recruited in Philadelphia by Colonel William H. Young, giving rise to one of the 3rd Cavalry's alternate names, "Young's Kentucky Light Cavalry." The Kentucky portion of the name was used as a tool to persuade the citizens of Kentucky to remain in the Union. They also bore the more official name of the 60th Pennsylvania Infantry.

The 3rd Cavalry reached Gettysburg around noon on July 2, 1863, the second day of the battle. The next day, they were on Brinkerhoff Ridge on the John Rummel farm, destined to become known as the East Cavalry Field. Lieutenant Colonel Edward S. Jones was in command in the absence of Colonel John McIntosh, who was commanding the 1st Brigade.

In this part of the battle, three brigades of cavalry under General J.E.B. Stuart launched a series of mounted charges, hoping to get through to the Union army's rear and take advantage of the diversion of their attention during Pickett's Charge.

Two Union brigades under Brigadier General David M. Gregg were dispatched to patrol Hanover and Low Dutch Roads in the event the Union army would need them in a retreat from Gettysburg. Gregg was supported by a brigade of Michigan cavalry under the command of General George Armstrong Custer. Those three brigades were called on to repulse Stuart,

William Edward Miller. *Congressional Medal of Honor Society, Mount Pleasant, South Carolina.*

who had graduated from West Point just a year ahead of Gregg. The two knew each other well.

Miller was under orders to hold his position and remain concealed in a nearby tree line near the Jacob Lott farm. On Stuart's final charge, the Southerners were met in force by Custer's 1st Michigan Cavalry. From his vantage point, Miller saw the violent collision. Horses turned end over end, and Miller later said J.E.B. Stuart that the sound of the battle was like the falling of timber. The din of battle was almost ear-piercing.

The flow of the clash went back and forth, with neither side gaining much of an advantage over the other. When Captain Hampton S. Thomas's New Jersey troops rushed into the Confederate left flank, Miller feared that Thomas might need support. Miller turned to his adjutant, Lieutenant William Brooke-Rowle, and said, "If you will back me up in case I am court-martialed for disobedience, I will order a charge."

With his adjutant's agreement, Miller launched his assault, throwing the surprised Confederates into confusion. Miller and his men poured through the Rebel left flank, separating the front and rear of their column. The Southerners shot Miller through his right arm but soon realized that the presence of Miller's men had the potential to cut off any chance they had to escape. The demoralized Rebels pulled back, and within minutes Stuart's assault was turned back. The threat to the Union rear was no more.

Miller mustered out on August 24, 1864, and he returned to the family farm for a short time before moving to Carlisle, Pennsylvania, where he opened a hardware store. In 1868, he remarried to Anna Bush. He became a state senator and was in great demand as a speaker.

Ironically, despite Miller's heroics, he did not merit so much as a brief mention in the official War Department record of the battle. On July 21, 1897, that slight was rectified when he was awarded the Medal of Honor, with the following citation:

> *Without orders, led a charge of his squadron upon the flank of the enemy, checked his attack, and cut off and dispersed the rear of his column.*

In May 1919, Miller suffered a stroke. He passed away in Carlisle on December 10, 1919, and was interred at Gettysburg National Cemetery.

He is one of only two Medal of Honor recipients in the cemetery. The other is Brevet Major General Charles Henry Tucker Collis, who earned his Medal at Fredericksburg.

John B. Mayberry, Private, Company F, 1st Delaware Infantry

Bernard McCarren, Private, Company C, 1st Delaware Infantry

It is interesting to note that one of our smallest states had three Medal of Honor recipients at Gettysburg. All three were from the 1st Delaware Infantry. The first, Captain James Parke Postles, was from Company A. The story of his dramatic dash through heavy fire to deliver a message is discussed in Part IV. The other two, Private John B. Mayberry (aka Maberry in some sources) of Company F and Private Bernard McCarren of Company C, took place simultaneously during Pickett's Charge. Both show that the importance of a captured flag is the flag itself rather than the act of capturing it.

Mayberry was born on December 17, 1841, in Smyrna, Delaware. Little is known of his civilian life other than that his wife's name was Susan and they had one daughter. He enlisted in the 1st Delaware's Company F on August 31, 1861.

McCarren was born in Ireland in 1830. The year he immigrated to the United States is unknown. He married Mary Ann Traynor in 1855, and they had two children, both of whom died young. When the Civil War began, McCarren enlisted in Company H of the 24th Pennsylvania Infantry for a three-month enlistment. At the end of his three months, he reenlisted, this time in Company C of the 1st Delaware Infantry.

The 1st Delaware arrived on the field early on July 2, the second day of the battle. Upon arrival, it took up a position near the Abraham Brian farm on Cemetery Ridge. The regiment saw a rapid turnover of commanders, beginning with Lieutenant Edward P. Harris, who was put under arrest later in the day for withdrawing from the buildings on the Bliss farm without authorization. He was replaced by Captain Thomas Bullock Hizard, who only served a very short time before being wounded so badly that he had to relinquish command to Lieutenant William Smith, who was killed on July 3 during the same action that Mayberry and McCarren earned their Medals. When Smith's body was retrieved, he was clutching a Confederate

John B. Mayberry. *Congressional Medal of Honor Society, Mount Pleasant, South Carolina.*

flag in his hand, thought to be the 5th Alabama Battalion. There were twenty-three Medals awarded at Gettysburg for capturing an enemy flag. Despite making the ultimate sacrifice, Smith was not one of them because nobody saw how he acquired the flag. With Smith's death, Lieutenant John Dent took command for the rest of the battle before relinquishing the duties back to Harris on July 4.

On July 3, the regiment waited with the rest of the Federal army as the fifteen thousand Confederates crossed the open fields of Pickett's Charge. Brigade commander Colonel Thomas Alfred Smyth ordered the men to refrain from firing until the gray line reached a point about fifty yards in front. Each man waited anxiously until the "Open fire!" command was given. Hearing the order, all stood up and fired as one, opening huge gaps in the Rebel line. The line slowed but did not stop until it was less than forty feet from the Union line, when it was driven back.

Seeing the Confederates pulling back, Lieutenant Smith led a countercharge over the stone wall. Smith was killed, apparently capturing the flag described previously. Mayberry was more fortunate, credited with capturing the flag of the 7th North Carolina Infantry. But did he really "capture" it? It is more likely that he picked it up off the battlefield, as there is no record of any kind of struggle or confrontation with the flag bearer, nor did anyone report seeing Mayberry specifically capture the flag. One account says that he seized the flag under fire, but that has not been corroborated.

In the same countercharge, McCarren "captured" the flag of the 13th Alabama Infantry, probably in a similar manner to Mayberry's flag capture, although some accounts say he also seized the flag under fire. The flag bearer and color guard were all believed to have been killed or wounded, so McCarren, and possibly Mayberry as well, most likely got the flag from the body of the flag bearer. However the two obtained the flags is not as important as the fact that the flags were now in the possession of the 1st Delaware Infantry.

Mayberry was later promoted to sergeant, and he suffered a head wound at the Battle of the Wilderness in May 1864. Following a stay in a Washington hospital, he was mustered out on July 15, 1865.

1st Delaware Infantry monument, representing Bernard McCarren. *Author photo.*

While he emerged from the battle unscathed, McCarren was also badly wounded on May 6, 1864, at the Battle of the Wilderness when a musket ball struck him and lodged in his scapula. He spent the next eight months recuperating in a hospital. He mustered out July 22, 1865, one week after Mayberry, and returned to Wilmington.

McCarren was awarded the Medal of Honor on December 1, 1864, for his actions that day in Gettysburg. Mayberry received his Medal five days later at a review at the Second Corps Headquarters at Peebles House near Petersburg, Virginia. It was presented to him by Major General George C. Meade.

With both receiving their medals for the same action, it is only fitting that both citations read the same:

> *Capture of flag.*

McCarren's medal is housed today in the National Archives and Records Administration in Washington. McCarren died of dysentery on June 20, 1870, in Wilmington, Delaware. He was laid to rest in the Old Cathedral All Saints Cemetery in Wilmington.

Mayberry turned to farming following his time in the army, and he continued farming at Pearson's Corner, Delaware, until 1912, when age forced him to quit. He moved to Dover, where he died on his eighty-first birthday, on December 17, 1922. He was buried at Glenwood Cemetery in Smyrna, Delaware.

William H. Raymond, Corporal, Company A, 108th New York Infantry

William Raymond was born on May 30, 1844, in Penfield, New York, and did not leave home until he enlisted. His schooling consisted of attendance in both summer and winter from the time he was seven years old until he was twelve. After that, he attended only in winter, using summers to work on a farm. On July 22, he enlisted in Company A of the 108th New York Infantry. Almost immediately, his new friends joked with him about his tall, lean stature. At Gettysburg, those jokes about being so thin would stop.

The 108th Infantry, also known as the Rochester Regiment, arrived at Gettysburg on July 2, 1863, and was positioned in Ziegler's Grove in support of the 1st U.S. Artillery's Battery I. The next morning, skirmishers were sent forward as a response to fire from Rebel skirmishers. Although most of the regiment enjoyed relative safety in the cover Ziegler's trees, the skirmishers had virtually no cover.

When the skirmishers, who only had the ammunition they carried out to the skirmish line with them, signaled that they were nearly out of ammunition, an officer called for volunteers to run for more. Raymond, acting as orderly sergeant, stood up. With heavy fire from both small weapons and artillery, nobody else chose to leave the cover of the trees.

William H. Raymond. *Congressional Medal of Honor Society, Mount Pleasant, South Carolina.*

Alone, Raymond began the mad dash through the rain of shells and bullets to the Union's main line, miraculously making it through unscathed. There he learned that brigade commander Colonel Thomas Alfred Smyth had been struck in the face by a shell fragment, and the 108th's Colonel Francis E. Pearce was now in command of the brigade. Pearce thanked Raymond for coming with the message that ammunition was needed and suggested that someone else could take it back, since Raymond had already risked his life once on the way over. Raymond thought otherwise and replied, "It might as well be me as anyone."

Placing the box on his shoulder because of its weight, he began the race back to the protection of the trees. Reaching safety, his friends crowded around him, pounding him on the back and telling him that he had done a great thing. It was then that the jokes about Raymond's thin stature ended. Although not one enemy bullet had touched him, his friends counted seven holes in his clothing.

Raymond survived the Battle of Gettysburg but became sick not long after. On August 4, he was placed in the camp hospital and then transferred to Armory Square Hospital in Washington on August 20. He would not be well enough to return to the regiment until December 10, 1863.

Five months later, at the Battle of the Wilderness, he was slightly wounded and taken prisoner. When he was released seven days later, he rejoined the regiment at Spotsylvania and was discharged with his regiment on May 28, 1865.

He returned to the Rochester area and resumed farming. He also married Olivia A. McOmber, and the couple would have two daughters. In the winter of 1865–66, he went west to Ohio and Indiana, where he worked on a railroad. Returning to New York in the spring of 1868, he worked in various jobs until his heroism at Gettysburg was rewarded.

In late 1895, his congressman, Henry C. Brewster, recommended him for the Medal of Honor. That Medal was awarded to him on March 10, 1896, with a citation reading:

> *Voluntarily and under a severe fire brought a box of ammunition to his comrades on the skirmish line.*

His newly found fame gained him a job as a clerk in the census bureau in Washington in 1900. He remained with the census bureau until his death on December 7, 1916. He was buried at Arlington National Cemetery

Alexander Stewart Webb, Brigadier General, Philadelphia Brigade

Alexander Stewart Webb was born into a military family in New York City on February 15, 1835. His father, a wealthy newspaper owner and U.S. minister to Brazil, was a former army officer, and his grandfather served on George Washington's staff during the Revolutionary War and was wounded at the Battle of Bunker Hill.

Webb attended West Point, graduating thirteenth in a class of thirty-four. Upon graduating, he was commissioned a brevet second lieutenant in the United States Regiments and was assigned to serve in Florida in the Seminole War. He then was appointed as an instructor of mathematics at West Point. In 1855, he married Anna Elizabeth Remsen. They would eventually be the parents of eight children.

When the Civil War began, Webb served at the First Battle of Bull Run, and at Malvern Hill on July 1, 1862, he set up a defensive line of artillery that was unsurmountable, gaining him significant recognition.

During the Battle of Chancellorsville, General George Meade placed Webb in command of a brigade, where he performed well in battle. He received special recognition in Meade's battle report for his intelligence and zeal.

Three days before the Battle of Gettysburg, Webb replaced Brigadier General Joshua T. Owen as commander of the Philadelphia Brigade, consisting of the 69th, 71st, 72nd and 106th Pennsylvania Infantries. While new to the brigade, he would soon gain their respect.

On July 2, Webb's Brigade was in position on Cemetery Ridge with the Second Corps. When Confederate Brigadier General Ambrose R. Wright's Brigade of Georgians came within range, Webb led the Philadelphia Brigade in a counterattack that pushed the Confederates back to Emmitsburg Road, capturing three hundred prisoners and reclaiming a Union battery that had been captured by the Rebels.

The next day, July 3, when the Confederate artillery attack began as a prelude to Pickett's Charge, Webb and the brigade were positioned in front of the Copse of Trees. With artillery shells exploding all around the brigade, he stood calmly in front of his line, leaning on his sword and smoking a cigar. He refused to seek shelter, even as the men under his command begged him to.

Alexander Stewart Webb. *Congressional Medal of Honor Society, Mount Pleasant, South Carolina.*

When the infantry assault got close to the Union line, Webb showed the characteristics of a competent leader when two companies of his 71st Pennsylvania began to fall back without having been ordered to do so. Webb called on the 72nd Pennsylvania Infantry to move forward, but it showed no inclination to follow the command. Webb rushed over to the regimental colors and attempted to take them from the color bearer, but the man was shot and went down. Soon every member of the color guard was either killed or wounded.

Seeing a company of Rebels breaching the Union line behind Confederate General Lewis Armistead, Webb abandoned further effort to cajole the 72nd Pennsylvania into action. Running between the two clashing lines, which were devolving into hand-to-hand fighting in some places, he raced toward his nearest regiment, the 69th Pennsylvania Infantry. Many of the assaulting Confederates, seeing a general officer so close, directed their fire toward him. One bullet struck him near the groin, but he reached the 69th Pennsylvania and directed its fire into the breaching Rebels.

Despite his painful wound, he continued directing fire even as more than half the 69th Pennsylvania became casualties, and eventually the assault was repulsed. General Meade, commander of the Union army at Gettysburg, said that Webb's action was not surpassed by any general on the field.

Webb was wounded again at Spotsylvania when he was shot in the head. That wound and the one he received at Gettysburg plagued him the rest of his life and were the reason he requested to be honorably discharged on December 31, 1870. Before retirement, he spent two years back at West Point, serving as principal assistant professor of geography, history and ethics.

From 1869 to 1902, Webb served as the second president of the City College of New York, retiring from that position when the effects of his war wounds proved to be too overwhelming.

On September 28, 1891, he was awarded the Medal of Honor for his actions at Gettysburg. The accompanying citation read:

> *Distinguished personal gallantry in leading his men forward at a critical period in the contest.*

The 1904 design of his Medal is at the West Point Museum.

General Webb died in Riverdale, New York, on February 12, 1911, at age seventy-six and was buried at the U.S. Military Academy Cemetery at West Point.

James Wiley, Sergeant, Company B, 59th New York Infantry

James Wiley was born in Ohio in 1835, and his early years were unremarkable. He enlisted into Company B of the 59th New York on September 20, 1861, and was mustered in sometime in November of that same year. Under the command of Colonel William Linn Tidball, the regiment's first assignment was the defense of Washington, where it remained for the next seven months.

Army life appeared to agree with Wiley. Except for being away from his family for the first time in his life, he began to consider reenlisting when his three-year enlistment was over. Nothing would change his mind over the next four months. The only thing resembling danger during that time came when the regiment was assigned to cover Pope's retreat to Washington at the end of August 1862, and even that turned out to be uneventful.

Then came Antietam, however. There the inexperienced 59th New York got off to a bad start in the West Woods. As the troops fired their first shots in anger, an officer began screaming at them to cease fire—they were firing into the 15th Massachusetts. Then, as the battle wore on, any thoughts of an easy army life disappeared when the regiment lost 8 officers among its 224 casualties.

Fredericksburg and Chancellorsville came next, and the 59th Infantry took heavy casualties in each; the Union army was defeated in both. Following the Fredericksburg fight, Colonel Tidball was discharged, and Lieutenant Colonel William Northedge took over command of the regiment. Two weeks later, the regiment took part in the infamous Mud March, leading to a great deal of complaining among the men about the competence of their leaders.

James Wiley captured a Confederate flag when the Southerners breached the Union defenses near the regiment's position, marked by the monument. *Author photo.*

Command changed once again in June when Northedge was forced to retire amid allegations of corruption and being drunk while on duty. His place was taken by Lieutenant Colonel Max A. Thoman, who would still be in command when the regiment reached Gettysburg.

On July 2, 1863, the badly depleted regiment was in position along Cemetery Ridge. It had suffered so many losses in its previous battles that the men had been consolidated into a small battalion of four companies less than a month before arriving at Gettysburg. Their force now totaled only 182 men, barely equivalent to two full-strength companies. Over the next several hours, they would assist in pushing back an assault by Confederate Brigadier General Ambrose R. Wright. Unnerved by the day's action, Wiley got little sleep that night.

Still in the same position on July 3, Wiley and his friends endured the Confederate bombardment that preceded Pickett's Charge. The very ground where they huddled behind a stone wall shook with the continuous shock from the Confederate guns. To a man, every one of the 59th New York would later agree that never had they experienced anything as terrifying.

Then the guns stopped. Except for the cries of the wounded, both man and beast, the battlefield was enveloped by an eerie silence. Before long, Wiley saw them, along with every other man on the Union line. Thousands of men in gray and butternut, materializing like ghosts through the smoke from the cannon fire on Seminary Ridge. The line was so long that Wiley couldn't see either end. And they marched as if on parade.

When the Federal artillery began firing, huge openings suddenly appeared in their ranks, openings that closed quickly and seemed to have little effect on their advancement. Filled with trepidation over what was about to come, Wiley couldn't help admiring the bravery he was witnessing.

The line reached the Emmitsburg Road, where they tore down the fences while under fire, then continued. In Wiley's mind, they were all coming directly at him. He gave little thought to the fact that every other Federal soldier was thinking the same about himself.

Finally, the order came to commence firing. Wiley fired, reloaded, fired again, reloaded, fired again—all without aiming. There was no need, the line of Rebels was now so close that he didn't need to aim; he couldn't miss at that distance. Some of his comrades only fired a few shots and then found themselves unable to reload. In their excitement they had forgotten to remove their ramrods before firing. The ramrods were somewhere out there, having been a part of the charge they had fired on their last volley.

Then the Rebels breached the stone wall. There was no longer time to reload. In the melee that ensued, Wiley saw a Confederate flag looming not far in his front. Rushing toward it, he was surprised that he wasn't being challenged until he realized that every man on both sides was so engrossed in the hand-to-hand fighting that was in progress that they only focused on their own part of the battle. Reaching the flag bearer, Wiley reached out and tore the banner from its staff. He immediately turned and began running to the Union line with his prize, the Confederate responsible for protecting that flag right behind him.

Reaching the line, he turned to confront his nemesis and noticed that the man wasn't there anymore. Wiley would not see him again. For the first time, Wiley looked at the flag he had just captured. It belonged to the 48th Georgia.

Wiley survived the Battle of Gettysburg and went on to fight at the Wilderness, Spotsylvania Court House, Cold Harbor and the Siege of Petersburg. He was captured during the fighting at Jerusalem Plank Road on June 22, 1864, and sent to Andersonville Prison. He died there on February 7, 1865, and was buried at Andersonville Prison Cemetery.

Two months before his death, on December 1, 1864, he was awarded the Medal of Honor, his citation reading:

> *Capture of flag of a Georgia regiment.*

His Medal, unseen by its recipient, is held at the National Archives and Records Administration in Washington.

George H. Dore, Sergeant, Company D, 126th New York Infantry

Jerry Wall, Private, Company B, 126th New York Infantry

Morris Brown Jr., Captain, Company A, 126th New York Infantry

Anyone who has been seriously and incorrectly accused of something has probably longed for the opportunity to avenge that slight at some point in their life. The men of the 126th New York Infantry felt the same as they went into battle at Gettysburg. Their chance was about to come.

These three men named here played prominent roles in correcting the slight against the regiment. George H. Dore was an Englishman, born on June 24, 1945, on the Isle of Wight. He was living in West Bloomfield, New York, when he enlisted at age seventeen.

Jerry Wall was born on July 1, 1941, in Geneva, New York, the hometown of the 126th New York. Orphaned at the age of four, Wall became known as "Little Jerry" or "Shorty" among the men of the 126th New York due to his five-foot-four and one-hundred-pound stature.

Morris Brown Jr., another New Yorker, was born in August 1842 in Hammondsport, New York. He was a student at Hamilton College when he decided to enlist.

So what was the stigma that the men of the regiment were carrying? It all had started at Harpers Ferry in September 1862. The regiment had never seen battle, and when the garrison fell during the Antietam Campaign, most of the terror-stricken men panicked and ran. Chased down by the Confederates, they became prisoners of war. In fact, more than twelve thousand Federal prisoners were taken that day, the largest single capture of Union troops of the war, a figure that would not be exceeded until twenty-two thousand Americans were captured by Japanese forces in World War II. The captives were paroled and sent to Annapolis, Maryland, then on to Camp Douglas in Chicago, where they spent the next two months guarding prisoners until they were exchanged on November 22, 1862. When word spread that they had run during the Harpers Ferry fighting, they began to be called the "Harpers Ferry Cowards." That stinging nickname was one they had lived with since then, and the entire regiment was anxious to do something to get rid of it.

On July 3, 1863, the 126th New York was on Cemetery Ridge, north of the Brian farm and just south of what is referred to as Cyclorama Drive today. They were part of the fishhook-shaped defensive line that extended from Little Round Top northward before curving toward Culp's Hill. The regiment was commanded by Colonel Eliakim Sherrill, who had taken over just one day earlier when Colonel George L. Willard was killed. Sherrill himself was destined to be mortally wounded within the next few hours during Pickett's Charge.

The regiment had just endured that nearly unbearable artillery attack, the hardest fire the regiment had ever experienced, and many of the men had fought the urge to run once again. Some later admitted to thinking that maybe they really were cowards. Now they watched as that impressive line of battle made its way toward them, banners flying magnificently in the breeze.

Their position placed them on the crest of a small hill, with no protection. They were perfectly outlined against the sky, making them precise targets for the Rebel guns. No more than 150 feet in front of the line, Morris Brown Jr. and the rest of Company A were deployed as skirmishers, unprotected on either side.

Then it started. First a scattered shot or two coming from a nervous Rebel as he moved toward the Yankees. Then a few more, and finally the entire line was firing. The Union line answered with a barrage of its own, and the battle was on. Company A began to pull back, reaching the line just as Colonel Sherrill came through on a gray horse. Almost immediately, the colonel was shot from his horse, dead before he hit the ground.

An artillery shell struck the color guard, killing or wounding them all and throwing the colors to the ground. The Rebels were getting close enough that the fallen flag was in danger of being captured. Dore, not even a citizen of the country whose army he had joined, knew the ramifications if that happened. Disregarding the danger, he rushed forward, placing himself between the two firing lines. With bullets zipping past from both directions, he scooped up the flag and returned it to the ranks.

Charging Rebels were now nearly to the crest of the hill. With men falling around him, Brown vowed that he would not be remembered as a coward. The Rebels had to be pushed back. Almost simultaneously with Lieutenant Samuel Wilson, he rushed toward the advancing Confederates. Several from Company A followed, and with bayonets slashing, the blue and gray met head on. Brown knew that there had to be an enemy flag bearer somewhere in the roiling mass of humanity surrounding him, and there it was. Shoving someone aside, so focused on the flag that he didn't know if it was friend or foe he assaulted, he made for the Rebel colors. Holding the barrel of his gun, he brought it down as hard as he could onto the Rebel's arm. The man screamed in pain and dropped the flag, whereupon Brown snatched it up much as Dore had done with the regimental colors. Brown's prize was soon identified as those of the 14th North Carolina.

For his part, Little Jerry Wall had no trouble spying another enemy flag. It was being carried by the largest man Wall had ever seen, a six-foot-ten bear of a man. Ignoring their eighteen-inch height difference, Wall rushed the flag bearer, leveled his gun on the man and demanded he surrender his prize. The man didn't know if Wall's gun was loaded or not, but the little man in front of him with the bayonet just inches from his throat looked determined. Reluctantly, the man relinquished the trophy to Wall and surrendered. The

George Dore saved the colors in front of the regiment's position, shown by their monument. Jerry Wall and Morris Brown captured flags in the same area. *Author photo.*

ownership of the flag was not recorded but was almost certainly another North Carolina regiment.

Shortly after, the assault collapsed, and the 126th was credited with capturing scores of prisoners. As the Confederates withdrew, cheers arose from the ranks of the New Yorkers. Those cheers grew even louder when General Alexander Hays took the captured flag from Brown and dragged it behind his horse. One of the battles inscribed on the flag was Harpers Ferry. The 126th New York would be called cowards no more.

Wall survived the war with no wounds, but Dore was wounded at Auburn, Virginia, on October 14, 1863. He survived that wound, and both mustered out in 1865. Brown was not as fortunate. He was killed on June 22, 1864, at Petersburg.

Dore and Wall were presented the Medal of Honor by Major General George G. Meade on December 6, 1864, at a review of the Second Corps Headquarters at Peebles House near Petersburg, Virginia. Dore's citation read:

> *The colors being struck down by a shell as the enemy were charging, this soldier rushed out and seized it, exposing himself to the fire of both sides.*

The citation for Wall was much simpler:

> *Capture of flag.*

Upon presenting Wall with his medal, Meade reportedly said, "Well done, little fellow."

Brown was later presented with a Medal of Honor as well. On March 6, 1869, his posthumous award contained a simple citation, identical to that of Jerry Wall:

> *Capture of flag.*

Dore died on February 8, 1927, at Hornell, New York. He was interred at Hope Cemetery in Hornell. Wall lived until July 28, 1930, when he died in Dansville, New York. He was buried at Dansville's Greenmount Cemetery. Brown's remains were laid to rest in Lake View Cemetery in Penn Yan, New York.

Wheelock Graves Veazey, Colonel, 16th Vermont Infantry

Wheelock Graves Veazey was born in Brentwood, New Hampshire, to Jonathan and Annie (Stevens) Veazey on December 5, 1835. As a youth he attended Phillips (Exeter) Academy, then Dartmouth College, graduating in 1859. The next year, he graduated from law school in Albany, New York, began practicing law in Springfield in 1860 and was admitted to the Vermont bar in December 1861.

In May 1861, he enlisted as a private into the 3rd Vermont Volunteers, was elected captain when the regiment formally organized and rose through the ranks until he became a lieutenant colonel. On June 22, 1861, despite the uncertainty of going to war, he married Julia A. Heard, with whom he would have four children.

In the fall of 1862, he was sent home to organize a new regiment. That regiment became the 16th Vermont, and on September 27, 1862, he was elected colonel of the nine-month regiment. He mustered out at the expiration of its term of enlistment.

As an enticement to get him to reenlist, General Winfield Scott Hancock offered him a rank of brigadier general, but health issues prevented Veazey from accepting. Later, as his health improved, he returned to the military, serving for a time on the staff of General William (Baldy) Smith. He also served as commander of various other regiments, and at Gettysburg he commanded the 16th Vermont Infantry, the regiment he organized and recruited.

There, on the evening of July 2, 1863, he was ordered to take his regiment, which had never seen battle action, and establish a picket line. It wasn't hard to tell they were new troops. Some of their movements were made timidly, with no sign of self-assurance. But the real giveaway were the uniforms—bright blue, with no signs of wear the battle-worn troops around them knew immediately—and some who remembered their first battle vowed to help them where they could. As it would turn out, no help would be needed.

Veazey's position placed him in the direct path of the route that would be taken by General George Pickett's Division. Thus, his troops had the unenviable position that became the first to be struck by the oncoming assault that would become known as Pickett's Charge. Veazey ordered his men to hold their ground initially against the Southern skirmishers. When the main lines drew nearer, however, he moved his troops back and to his right, taking a position alongside the 13th Vermont. In doing so, he passed the wounded General Winfield Scott Hancock, who reportedly said to him,

"That's right, Colonel, go in and give 'em hell on the flank." The new position placed him where the exposed flank of the Rebels would pass in his front. When it ultimately did, the two Vermont regiments inflicted horrendous damage onto Pickett's right flank.

Wheelock Graves Veazey. *Congressional Medal of Honor Society, Mount Pleasant, South Carolina.*

As the Confederate line broke down, the 16th Vermont troops scattered and were exuberantly taking prisoners who had lost their will to fight. Veazey quickly gathered them back into position when he spied the brigades of Brigadier General Edward Perry and Brigadier General Cadmus Wilcox moving along a similar path. The Vermonters then repeated their attack on the flanks, ripping into the Confederate ranks and taking several hundred prisoners.

Later that year, Veazey returned to Vermont in poor health. After recovering, he returned to the practice of law. Over the next several years, he served as a reporter of the Vermont Supreme Court, preparing nine volumes of the Vermont Reports. He also served as a state senator, judge and reviser of the Vermont state laws. In 1879, he received an appointment as judge of the Vermont Supreme Court, a position he held until 1889, when he resigned to accept an appointment to the Interstate Commerce Commission.

From 1879 until 1891, he also served as a trustee of his alma mater, Dartmouth College, and he became a delegate to the Republican National Convention that nominated Rutherford B. Hayes for president. He also was elected commander-in-chief of the Grand Army of the Republic.

On September 8, 1891, he was awarded the Medal of Honor for his gallantry on July 3, 1863. The accompanying citation read:

> *Rapidly assembled his regiment and charged the enemy's flank; charged front under heavy fire, and charged and destroyed a Confederate brigade, all this with new troops in their first battle.*

Veazey passed away on March 22, 1898, and received a hero's burial at Arlington National Cemetery.

Note: This section was adapted from one that originally appeared on the website of the Congressional Medal of Honor Society.

Marshall Sherman, Private, Company C, 1st Minnesota Infantry

From time to time, battlefield accounts differ as to how an event unfolded. Sometimes it is because memories become clouded after a while or because the inevitable flow of adrenalin causes the brain to process things differently among several people. Or, unfortunately, accounts may differ simply because of jealousy. However it happened for Private Marshall Sherman, his story provides a perfect example of this.

Sherman was born in 1823 in Burlington, Vermont. Beyond that, not much is known about his childhood or his parents. At some point, he moved to Minnesota, where he is known to have been a house painter. He also entered into a partnership with James McClellan Boal. Boal was an artist, trader and politician, as well as a house and sign painter, so it is surmised that the partnership had something to do with painting houses, although that is not documented.

On April 29, 1861, Marshall Sherman mustered in to the 1st Minnesota. That date would indicate that he was one of the first Minnesotans to enlist in the Union army. He would go on to fight in such battles as Bull Run, Ball's Bluff, the Seven Days, Antietam and Gettysburg.

The heroic charge by the 1st Minnesota on July 2 was documented in the section on Corporal Henry D. O'Brien earlier in this part. Having been with his company on detached duty, Sherman would not have been a part of the charge. Hearing about it around the campfire that evening made him sorrowful for his lost friends, but he was also a bit envious of those who had the opportunity to be a part of it. His turn was about to come.

On July 3, the regiment woke to the sound of gunfire near Culp's Hill on its right. As the sun was still rising, the men moved to their designated positions in the Union line. Once there, they made a crude barricade of fence rails, cobble stones and their dirt-filled knapsacks. Around 1:00 p.m. came the artillery duel, and the grizzled veterans of the 1st Minnesota knew what was to follow. An infantry attack always came after a preliminary artillery assault, and the barrage they had just endured had been like none they had ever experienced, so the infantry offensive promised to be a big one.

And just as every one of the Minnesotans knew would happen, there they were. Three lines deep, they advanced without hesitation, closing their ranks when Union artillery found its mark. When the line reached a point about one hundred yards in front, the order was given to begin firing. Men in gray uniforms began to fall with regularity, but instead of slowing or retreating, they changed their pace to double-quick.

When the Vermont troops enfiladed the Confederate flank, it also served to divert the main body of the Confederate line slightly to their left. They pushed back the 71st Pennsylvania and poured over Cushing's Battery. By this time, they had passed the position held by the 1st Minnesota, which wheeled and attacked the right flank of the Rebel line. An order to charge was screamed out, and the Minnesotans rushed to the Angle, where the attack was heaviest. Once again, the fighting was man to man. At some point in this part of the struggle, Sherman encountered the 28th Virginia flag bearer and wrestled the flag from him, taking the man prisoner in the process.

Marshall Sherman stands with the flag he captured. *Congressional Medal of Honor Society, Mount Pleasant, South Carolina.*

Here is where the accounts diverge, as Private David Bond remembered it differently. In his version, Bond insists that the flag was simply leaning against a tree. He said that he ran toward the tree hoping to grab the flag, but Sherman had been closer and got there first. He said there had been no struggle and that the flag was sitting there for the taking. Whose story is accurate? We will probably never know, but there was no dispute that Sherman brought a prisoner in while carrying the man's flag. With Bond being the only man who disputed Sherman's version, regimental records favored Sherman's account, and they made no official mention of the disagreement.

Sherman remained in the 1st Minnesota until he was wounded and lost his leg in a skirmish near Petersburg, Virginia, in 1864, at which time he was mustered out of the army. He returned to St. Paul and returned to relative obscurity. He never married and had no descendants.

On December 1, 1864, shortly after mustering out, he learned that his actions had earned him the Medal of Honor. His citation reported:

> *Capture of flag of 28th Virginia Infantry (C.S.A.).*

On April 19, 1896, Marshall Sherman took his last breath. He was buried at Oakland Cemetery in St. Paul, Minnesota. The flag he captured was displayed at his funeral.

William Wells, Major, 2nd Battalion, 1st Vermont Cavalry

Born in Waterbury, Vermont, on December 14, 1837, William Wells was one of a family of ten children, nine of them boys. His parents, William and Elizabeth, encouraged William in his education, sending him to Kimball Union Academy in Meriden, New Hampshire. He used that background to survey a county map of Caledonia County using an odometer.

When the Civil War began, he enlisted as a private in the 1st Vermont Cavalry, eventually rising to colonel and regimental commander. On July 3, with Pickett's Charge already repulsed and the Confederate cavalry defeated at East Cavalry Field, Brigadier General Judson Kilpatrick ordered a senseless cavalry charge against entrenched Confederate troops near Big Round Top. The charge had no hope of success, going over a rock-strewn field on horseback and through heavy timber. Kilpatrick had already attained the unenviable nickname of "Kill Cavalry" for many of his ill-advised previous orders, and history would forever link him to this charge as evidence of his ineptitude.

When Captain Elon Farnsworth, commander of the 1st Brigade, 3rd Division, Cavalry Corps, protested to Kilpatrick that such a charge was foolhardy and had no chance of succeeding, Kilpatrick accused him of being a coward. Farnsworth relented, and he made the charge with Major Wells leading the 2nd Battalion of the 1st Vermont Cavalry. The location of this charge would become known as the South Cavalry Field.

The charge crossed Plum Run and followed along a stone wall, reaching the spur of Big Round Top. Turning north toward the town, they passed behind Alabama regiments commanded by Brigadier General Evander Law. As the cavalry passed, Law's men turned and fired on them. Farnsworth was killed, but somehow Wells was uninjured. Upon Farnsworth's death, Wells took command of the survivors, continued the charge and ultimately led them safely back to Union lines.

Just days after Gettysburg, Wells was wounded by a saber at the Battle of Boonsboro. He was wounded a second time in September 1863 at Culpeper Court House in a charge that resulted in his men capturing a Confederate gun.

In March 1864, he commanded a cavalry detachment on Dahlgren's raid on Richmond. Three months later, he commanded a cavalry brigade in the Shenandoah Valley and at the Battles of 3rd Winchester and Cedar Creek. In 1865, he was appointed brevet brigadier general, and on March 30, 1865, he was appointed brevet major general of volunteers for gallant and meritorious service. On the personal recommendations of Generals Phil Sheridan and George Custer, he was commissioned a brigadier general on May 16, 1865, and on the morning of Lee's surrender at Appomattox Court House, Wells had already started on his final charge when he was stopped by Custer. Sheridan would say that Wells represented his ideal cavalry officer. Wells received more promotions and was one of the most decorated soldiers from Vermont in the Civil War.

William Wells. *Hall of Valor.*

A statue to Wells sits at the approximate starting point of the ill-fated cavalry charge on July 3. A replica of the statue sits in a park in his hometown of Burlington, Vermont.

On September 8, 1891, Wells received the Medal of Honor, accompanied by a citation that read:

> *Led the second battalion of his regiment in a daring charge.*

Wells died on April 29, 1892, in New York City and was buried at Lakeview Cemetery in Burlington.

John E. Clopp, Private, Company F, 71st Pennsylvania Infantry

Most of us have learned over time that making generalities can be dangerous, that it is folly to assume all individuals are the same in an organization that has a questionable reputation. The story of John Clopp illustrates the danger of making such assumptions.

John Clopp was born in Philadelphia in 1845, and except for earning the Medal of Honor, little is known about any stage of his life or his military career. Muster records of the 71st Pennsylvania Infantry show a John E. Clopp mustering in on February 28, 1864, which is after the Battle of Gettysburg. The regiment's records also showed a Tobias Clopp and a Frederick Clopp, but even the John E. Clopp, if it is the same John E. Clopp who earned the Medal, is not shown as earning the award, nor does the official battle

John E. Clopp wrestled a Confederate flag from its bearer in fighting near the Angle, where the regiment's monument sits. *Author photo.*

report of the regiment. The story of his action is pieced together from other regimental sources and is open to conjecture.

Much more is known about the 71st Pennsylvania. At the onset of the Civil War, many residents on the West Coast wished to have a presence in the Eastern Theater. However, distance and the lack of a railroad to connect the two coasts made that impractical. As an alternative, they approached U.S. Senator Edward D. Baker and requested that he organize a brigade in California's name. Baker agreed to the proposal, and he, in turn, spoke about the plan with President Lincoln. In April 1861, Lincoln commissioned Baker to organize a brigade in Philadelphia that would be credited to California.

With Lincoln's approval, Baker organized a brigade consisting of the 1st, 2nd, 3rd and 5th California Infantries. Baker would be the brigade's commander. The brigade saw its first action at the Battle of Ball's Bluff, near Leesburg, Virginia. Fighting against the 8th Virginia Infantry, Baker was mortally wounded.

With Baker's death, Pennsylvania took ownership of the California Brigade, and the 1st California Volunteer Infantry became the 71st Pennsylvania Infantry.

Commanded by Colonel R. Penn Smith, the 71st Pennsylvania was positioned near the Angle on the Gettysburg battlefield on July 3, 1863. The regiment played a prominent role the day before in turning back a Confederate offensive and assisting in the recapture of a Union gun. That would not be the case on this day, with a few exceptions. Clopp's actions were among those exceptions.

The regiment was split into two segments, with one along a stone wall beside the 69th Pennsylvania and the other about fifty yards behind and slightly to the right. When Cushing's Battery was in danger of being overrun during Pickett's Charge, about fifty men from the 69th and 71st Infantries rushed to the battery and continued to work the guns that were still operational. Based on what took place here with the 9th Virginia Infantry, it is likely that Clopp was part of this contingent.

When the Confederates breached the stone wall, the left portion of the 71st Infantry collapsed and retreated. Brigadier General Alexander Webb tried desperately to regroup them and move them forward, to no avail. Seeing the collapse, the Rebels unleashed a loud yell and rushed to follow their General Lewis Armistead, who had reached a Union gun and placed his hand on it. Armistead subsequently fell, mortally wounded, and the attack was beaten back.

In the brutal hand-to-hand fighting that took place between the time the wall was breached and the time Armistead was wounded, Clopp and the flag bearer from the 9th Virginia got into a tussle over the Virginian's flag. After a brief struggle, Clopp managed to wrestle the flag away.

Within minutes the Southerners began to retreat. The ground on the Union side of the wall was covered with wounded and dead from both sides. Later accounts described the area as strewn with "disabled artillery, muskets, canteens, knapsacks, and all the munitions of war."

The Confederate dead were buried where they fell, with a large sign posted at one end of the mass grave saying, "The remains of the Ninth and Seventeenth Virginia Regiments. A worthy foe."

Just as Clopp's early life and military service are obscure, so was his life after mustering out. What is known is that on February 2, 1865, he received the Medal of Honor, with a citation saying:

Capture of flag of 9th Virginia Infantry (C.S.A.), wresting it from the color bearer.

Obviously, Clopp returned to Philadelphia after he was discharged because he died there on April 6, 1866. He was buried at Lawnview Cemetery in Rockledge, Pennsylvania.

GEORGE GREENVILLE (GRENVILLE) BENEDICT, SECOND LIEUTENANT, COMPANY C, 12TH VERMONT INFANTRY

George Benedict was born in Burlington, Vermont, on December 10, 1826, to George and Eliza (Dewey) Benedict, one of four sons in the family. He graduated from the University of Vermont with honors in 1847 and obtained his master's degree in 1850. He married Mary Anne Kellogg on October 27, 1853. That same year, he became co-editor and publisher of the *Burlington Daily Free Press* with his father. He then served as president of the Vermont and Boston Telegraph Company from 1869 until 1863.

In August 1862, he enlisted into Company C of the 12th Vermont Infantry as a private for a nine-month enlistment. Company C would also be known as the Howard Guards. In January 1863, he was promoted to second lieutenant and aide-de-camp on the staff of General George Stannard, commander of the 2nd Vermont Brigade. When the Battle of Gettysburg began, he was sent on the first day of fighting to let the division commander know that the brigade was on its way. As such, he had the honor of being the first man of the brigade to reach the Gettysburg battlefield. The next day, he assisted the repositioning of the Union line after Sickles was pushed out of the Peach Orchard.

On July 3, the third day of the battle, with the Confederate artillery attack in full swing, Stannard used Benedict to place his regiments along the battle line. As described earlier in the discussion of Colonel Wheelock Veazey's actions, after the 13th and 16th Vermont Infantries attacked the flank of the advancing Confederates in Pickett's Charge, they had scattered to gather prisoners. When the next column appeared out of the smoke, Stannard dispatched Benedict to gather the men and reform them into a position of another flank attack.

Benedict dashed off through heavy grape and canister fire to deliver the order to the officers of both regiments and then began directing the Vermonters back to their original positions in preparation for the next wave of Rebels, walking along the line with his back to the enemy fire as he straightened the line. When some of the inexperienced men showed signs of panic, he calmed them and led them back to the line. When the battle ended, he positioned the brigade's picket line and then wrote an account of the battle for his newspaper, something he did regularly throughout his nine months in the army.

George Greenville Benedict. *Congressional Medal of Honor Society, Mount Pleasant, South Carolina.*

Following the conclusion of his enlistment, he returned home to Burlington, where, in 1866, he was made assistant inspector general of Vermont, with the rank of major. He was elected to the Vermont Senate from 1869 to 1871 and served as secretary of the Corporation of the University of Vermont and State Agricultural College from 1865 to 1879.

In 1879, he was appointed by Vermont Governor Redfield Proctor to the position of state military historian. In that capacity, he wrote two volumes of *Vermont in the Civil War*, a work that many historians have called the most readable of all the states' histories of the war. In 1880, he was elected to the board of trustees of the University of Vermont.

Throughout the years following his mustering out of service, he was active in various military organizations and served as an officer in many of them. By the time he retired as editor of the *Burlington Daily Free Press*, he was recognized as the dean of Vermont journalism.

On June 27, 1892, he was awarded the Medal of Honor for his actions on the third day at Gettysburg. His citation told the story:

> *Passed through a murderous fire of grape and canister in delivering order and re-formed the crowded line.*

On April 8, 1907, he died in Camden, North Carolina. His body was brought back to Burlington for burial at that city's Green Mount Cemetery.

Oliver P. Rood, Private, Company B, 20th Indiana Infantry

The very act of earning a Medal of Honor requires some action above and beyond the call of duty. Thus, in nearly all cases, that action is well documented simply because it stands out. On at least one such occasion, however, such was not the case, and while the story behind Oliver Rood's actions to earn the Medal are known, many of the details remain shrouded in mystery.

Oliver Rood was born in Frankfort, Kentucky, in 1844. As with many Civil War Medal of Honor recipients, little was recorded about his childhood or his family. His name first appears on August 30, 1862, when he enlisted in the 14th Indiana Infantry out of Vigo County, Indiana. His enlistment was for a three-year term.

His Medal of Honor citation, awarded December 1, 1864, plainly states:

> *Capture of flag of 21st North Carolina Infantry (C.S.A.).*

The date of the action is July 3, 1863, and the regiment he was with, according to the citation, was the 20th Indiana Infantry. This is where the mystery begins.

To start with, Rood was not in the 20th Indiana in 1863, when the Battle of Gettysburg was fought. As noted, he enlisted in the 14th Indiana, and records show that he was still in that regiment until June 6, 1864, nearly a full year, when he then transferred to the 20th Indiana.

To carry the mystery further, although the 20th Indiana was at Gettysburg, it was not engaged on July 3. On July 2, the regiment fought on Houck's Ridge and suffered 152 casualties, including 32 men who were killed. Two of those killed were officers, including the regiment's colonel, John Wheeler. The regiment was in such sorry shape after the Houck's Ridge fighting that it was held in reserve on July 3.

The 21st North Carolina, meanwhile, was heavily engaged on East Cemetery Hill on July 2, a considerable distance from Houck's Ridge, where the 20th Indiana was fighting. When the 21st North Carolina pulled back, its color bearer was killed. In the confusion of the withdrawal, it is likely that nobody took the flag along, possibly because it was hidden under the color bearer's body.

Coincidentally, the 14th Indiana, Oliver Rood's regiment, was also engaged on East Cemetery Hill the evening of July 2, and its color bearer was also killed. The regiment remained on East Cemetery Hill until the end of the battle on July 3.

Oliver Rood most likely gained possession of the 21st North Carolina flag in this area of East Cemetery Hill. *Author photo.*

Nobody has disputed that it was Rood who somehow came into possession of the 21st North Carolina's flag. By piecing together the actions of the 14th and 20th Indiana Infantries and those of the 21st North Carolina's, it is most likely that Rood found the flag sometime early on July 3, and it is simply a recordkeeping error that credited his find to the 20th Indiana, the regiment he was with on the date his Medal was awarded. The recommendation for the Medal that was sent to the War Department's Adjutant General's office on November 28, 1864, by Assistant Adjutant General E.D. Townsend showed Rood as being a member of the 20th Indiana, which he was by that time, and that error appears to have carried through all subsequent references.

On August 12, 1880, Rood wrote an open letter to all veterans of the Second Corps that appeared in the *Brownstown (IN) Banner*. In that letter, he endorsed General Winfield Scott Hancock for president and condemned what he referred to as malicious slander that had been directed at Hancock.

Rood died on June 1, 1885, in Nashville and was buried at Mount Olivet Cemetery in that city.

JOHN G. MILLER, CORPORAL, COMPANY G, 8TH OHIO INFANTRY

JAMES RICHMOND, PRIVATE, COMPANY F, 8TH OHIO INFANTRY

Those who have read this book from the beginning have no doubt noticed the emphasis that was placed on capturing a flag during the Civil War. The 8th Ohio Infantry had the honor of capturing three Confederate flags, all in the same action, and one of its members did the unthinkable by capturing *two* flags.

John G. Miller was born sometime in August 1841 in southeastern Germany, in Bavaria. His family immigrated to the United States and settled in Fremont, Ohio, where John grew up.

James Richmond was born in Maine in 1843 but was living in Toledo while Miller was growing up about thirty-five miles away. Both had uneventful lives until April 15, 1861. On that date, President Abraham Lincoln called for 75,000 volunteers to help put down a rebellion by several southern states. Northern states were asked to furnish a number of men in proportion to each state's population, and Ohio was asked to furnish thirteen regiments of 780 men each.

Few thought that it would take very long to end the Rebellion, and Ohio's regiments were formed as three-month regiments. On April 28, 1861, the 8th Ohio Infantry was organized. When it became apparent that the Rebellion was going to last longer than three months, the regiment was reorganized on July 8, 1861, this time for three years. Suddenly, John G. Miller and James Richmond were soldiers.

The first battle for the 8th Ohio came on March 22, 1862, the Battle of Kernstown. Both young men overcame the fear that every soldier feels in their first battle and did well. Miller did well enough to earn a promotion to corporal.

The regiment then engaged in several skirmishes over the next several months, all leading to the bloodiest day in American history, September 17, 1862. That day saw the regiment at Antietam, a battle in which James Richmond was slightly wounded at the Sunken Road.

On July 2, 1863, the regiment, commanded by Lieutenant Colonel Franklin Sawyer, was posted as skirmishers along Emmittsburg Road, near today's Long Lane across from the Brian farm. The men camped there overnight and were still there on July 3 when the Confederate artillery bombardment began. From that position, somewhat isolated from the main body of the Union line, they watched as Longstreet's Assault, more commonly called Pickett's Charge, began to advance.

John G. Miller and James Richmond earned their Medals of Honor in action near the 8th Ohio Infantry monument. *Author photo.*

As Colonel John Brockenbrough's Virginia Brigade drew closer, it became increasingly apparent that its northern flank was vulnerable. The 8th Ohio watched patiently as the Virginians resolutely approached. Then the order to charge was given. The regiment rose as one and attacked. With their eyes fixed on the stone wall ahead of them, Brockenbrough's men failed to see the Ohioans until they crashed into their flank. In short order, the Virginians were in disarray, and they began to fall back.

The Ohio troops then turned their attention to Major General Isaac Trimble's Division, striking its flank as well. With the attack coming from the side, the Southerners became confused. As was happening along the length of the Union line, the Confederates found themselves in deadly hand-to-hand fighting. It was here that Corporal John Miller killed the color guard from the 34th North Carolina Infantry and captured that regiment's flag.

With so many of their comrades either falling or being taken prisoner, it soon became apparent to Trimble's men that Pickett's Charge had failed. Reluctantly, painfully, they began the painful return to Seminary Ridge.

After a quick regrouping, the regiment rushed into the ranks of Armistead's Brigade. In fierce fighting near the Angle, Miller helped capture the flag bearer for the 38th Virginia Infantry, taking his flag and becoming the only known Ohioan to capture two flags.

At some point in the struggle, James Richmond left his mark on history, taking possession of a Confederate flag from an unknown regiment. It is not recorded whether he accomplished the feat in the first or second part of the action.

Both Miller and Richmond survived the Battle of Gettysburg. On December 1, 1864, both were awarded with the Medal of Honor. Both citations were understatements of what the two had accomplished. Miller's citation read:

> *Capture of two flags.*

Richmond's was nearly identical:

> *Capture of flag.*

Richmond's citation was awarded posthumously. On May 12, 1864, he was mortally wounded at Spotsylvania, passing away on June 3, 1864, after spending three painful weeks at Mount Pleasant Hospital in Washington. He was one of the earliest Civil War casualties to be buried at Arlington National Cemetery.

Miller eventually became a sergeant and was mustered out July 13, 1864. He died on June 11, 1909, and was interred at St. Mary's Cemetery in Champaign, Illinois.

EDMUND RICE, MAJOR, 19TH MASSACHUSETTS INFANTRY

Born on December 2, 1842, in Brighton, Massachusetts, to Moses and Eliza (Damon) Rice, Edmund Rice attended Norwich University in Vermont, finishing in 1856 but not receiving his degree until 1874. He became an apprentice on a clipper ship, returning home to become a surveyor for his father.

On August 22, 1861, he enlisted in the 14th Massachusetts with the rank of captain. When the unit was disbanded later in the year, he enlisted in the 19th Massachusetts, where he became commander of Company F. On September 7, 1862, he was promoted to major. By the time he reached Gettysburg, he had fought in nine battles, including Fredericksburg and Antietam. He was battle tested.

Around dawn on July 2, the regiment reached the battlefield under the command of Colonel Arthur F. Devereux. The men rested most of the day until about 5:00 p.m., when they were ordered to move in support of General Andrew Humphreys's Division. With little specific direction, the two regiments lay down and let the retreating Third Corps pass. They then rose up and delivered a volley into the pursuing Confederates, capturing several prisoners in the process. With their captives in tow they returned to their starting point, where they spent the night waiting for the attack that was almost sure to come their way the next day.

The morning of July 3 was relatively quiet, and Rice and the regiment thought that the anticipated Rebel assault may not happen. Then, the sound of a signal cannon came from the opposite ridge at about 1:00 p.m. It was immediately followed by the largest barrage of cannon fire any of them had ever heard. The very ground shook, and the men pressed as close to the ground as they could get, with most of the shots passing overhead. However, some found their mark. As Rice watched in horror, one of the early shots struck Lieutenant S.S. Robinson directly, cutting him nearly in two and killing him instantly.

When the two-hour salvo ended, the Confederate infantry took over, marching through the Union's artillery fire toward the Union line. As the gray-clad figures drew closer, the line on the 19th Massachusetts's right began to crumble. Seeing the danger of the line being breached, Rice turned and waved his arm overhead, pointing toward the approaching battle flags. "Follow me," he shouted to his men.

Leading the way, Rice looked back over his shoulder and saw that his men were all following behind him, bolstered by parts of the 7th Michigan

Edmund Rice was badly wounded leading a countercharge against Pickett's Charge on July 3, 1863. *Congressional Medal of Honor Society, Mount Pleasant, South Carolina.*

Infantry and the 42nd New York Infantry. As the one leading the charge, Rice was the first to contact the Confederates, and within seconds he was wounded. Refusing to relinquish command, he continued directing his men, buying sufficient time for the line to the 19th's right to reorganize. The entire line held, and the attack was beaten back. Pickett's Charge, and the Confederacy's hopes to defeat the Union army on its own ground, was over.

Under Rice's command, the 19th was responsible for capturing four stands of colors. The four men of the 19th who took the colors all were awarded the Medal of Honor for their actions. The actions of the four—Private John H. Robinson, Corporal Joseph H. DeCastro, Sergeant Benjamin H. Jellison and Sergeant Benjamin Falls—are described earlier in this part.

Rice recovered from his wound and survived the Battle of Gettysburg. He was promoted to lieutenant colonel on February 28, 1864, and commanded his regiment through several more battles. On May 12, 1864, however, he was wounded again and taken captive at the Battle of Spotsylvania Court House. While being moved southward to an unknown prison, he cut through the door of the freight car he had been placed in, jumping out with the train moving an estimated fifteen miles per hour. Traveling mostly at night, he reached the safety of Union lines twenty-three days later. Before being sent back to the 19th Massachusetts, he was promoted to colonel on July 28, 1864.

Rice returned to the regiment a few weeks later and continued to lead it through several more battles, receiving a third wound before Robert E. Lee surrendered. Following that surrender, Rice returned to civilian life on June 30, 1865.

He married Annie Clark Dutch on August 30, 1866. The two would have one daughter before Annie died of tuberculosis at age twenty. Rice returned to military service, joining the 40th Infantry, and he was credited with inventing several military tools. In 1881, he remarried, this time to Elizabeth Huntington, in Cincinnati.

Rice's unusual gravestone marks his final resting place at Arlington National Cemetery. *Author photo.*

On October 6, 1891, Rice was awarded the Medal of Honor. His citation credited him with

> *Conspicuous bravery on the third day of the battle on the countercharge against Pickett's division where he fell severely wounded within the enemy's lines.*

Remaining in the army, he took part in the Indian Wars, the Spanish-American War and the Philippine-American War before returning to the United States in July 1901, his health deteriorating. He retired on August 14, 1903, as a brigadier general.

On July 20, 1906, Rice died while relaxing in a hammock in Boston. Massachusetts showed its appreciation for what he had done for the country by having his body lie in state in the Hall of Flags of the statehouse before being transported to Arlington National Cemetery for burial. Second wife Elizabeth was buried with him in 1919.

Rice's grave is adorned with one of the more unique markers in Arlington, a large boulder with a three-foot bronze replica of his Medal affixed.

Alonzo Cushing, First Lieutenant, Battery A, 4th U.S. Light Artillery

An ancient Greek once wrote, "The mills of the Gods grind slowly." Henry Wadsworth Longfellow modernized the words a bit when he wrote his famous poem "Retribution," writing, "Though the mills of God grind slowly; Yet they grind exceeding small."

Whichever version you prefer, the words refer to the idea that things may happen slowly, but eventually there will be results. Nothing illustrates that better than the story of Alonzo Cushing.

Cushing was born in Delafield, Waukesha County, Wisconsin, on January 19, 1841, to Milton Buckingham and Mary Barker (Smith) Cushing. He was one of seven siblings plus a half sibling, and three of his brothers also served during the Civil War. While he was still just a young boy, the family moved to Fredonia, New York. In 1856, he was nominated by Congressman Francis Smith Edwards for an appointment to West Point. He graduated in 1861, twelfth in his class of thirty-four, and spent time in a number of assignments before receiving a field assignment to the 4th U.S. Light Artillery. Most of those in his battery had transferred in from infantry regiments, and Cushing spend a significant amount of time training them in military discipline and artillery techniques.

On July 2, 1863, Cushing and his battery set up on Cemetery Ridge near the Copse of Trees, at a point on the face of the ridge just above where two stone walls met. Their juncture would become known as the Angle. The morning of July 3 found them in that same location, facing across a long open field toward Seminary Ridge. The morning passed slowly without much happening, with Cushing's men engaging in a short artillery duel with some Confederate guns on Seminary Ridge. There was no damage to either side.

When the Southern artillery opened fire early in the afternoon, Cushing's men jumped to their feet, caught by surprise by the suddenness of the cannonade. Within minutes they were returning fire. For reasons unknown to Cushing, the Confederate fire seemed to be aimed directly at his battery, and some of the Southern fire was finding its target. A limber chest blew up, killing or wounding several members of the crew. A wheel on a cannon carriage collapsed, knocking the piece out of service. The crew started to abandon the piece, stopping only when Cushing drew his pistol and threatened to shoot anyone who ran. A spare wheel was brought up and installed, placing the gun back in operation.

By the time the Southern barrage ended, Cushing's Battery had been decimated. Only two cannons were serviceable, although that didn't really matter. Cushing, who had been hit in the shoulder by shell fragments, didn't have enough men to operate them. Ignoring the pain from his wound, he asked for permission from General Alexander Webb to move his two usable guns closer to the Angle, next to the 69th Pennsylvania Infantry. With Webb's blessing, Cushing and the remaining men from his crew moved a gun and piled extra canister rounds, similar to a cannon-sized shotgun shell, next to the gun.

Alonzo Cushing, recipient of the last Civil War Medal of Honor. *Congressional Medal of Honor Society, Mount Pleasant, South Carolina.*

Union artillery soon opened huge gaps in the oncoming lines. When the Southerners came within range, Union infantry began to fire. The combination of musket fire and cannon fire took a heavy toll, but still the Rebels came. Cushing's Battery joined in the carnage, Cushing personally directing every shot. He was wounded a second time in the groin and abdomen, and an officer ordered him to the rear. However, with only a partial crew already, Cushing refused, opting to stay and fight. Sergeant Frederick Fuger held his lieutenant upright, and with Cushing now too weak to shout out commands, Fuger relayed his orders to the rest of the crew members.

Switching to double canister rounds as the line got closer, Battery A's two guns tore one opening after another in the ranks. Now they were only a few feet apart. Cushing knew that he only had time now for one more shot. Trying to make himself heard above the roar of the battle, he informed Fuger that he was only going to be able to fire once more. Before he could pull the lanyard, he was wounded for the third time by a Rebel bullet that passed through his mouth and exited through the back of his skull, killing him instantly. His lifeless body dropped across the gun trail.

Fuger was awarded a Medal of Honor for his actions, and his story appears earlier in this part. Cushing received a posthumous promotion to brevet lieutenant colonel. His remains were transported to West Point, where he was laid to rest at the Military Academy's cemetery. His grieving mother, Mary, chose the inscription on his headstone:

Faithful unto Death.

Nearly 125 years later, back in Delafield, Wisconsin, on property once owned by Cushing's father, private citizen Margaret Zerwekh often wondered why Cushing had never been awarded the Medal of Honor. She began a personal campaign, sending a letter in 1987 to Senator William Proxmire. She later began writing similar letters to Congressman Ron Kind. For fifteen years, she collected a stack of form letters from various officials, none offering hope of any such award for Cushing. Finally, in 2002, Wisconsin Senator Russ Feingold notified Zerwekh that he agreed with her, and he nominated Cushing for the belated Medal of Honor. It would be eight more years before the U.S. Army approved the nomination. Still, there was more to be done. Congress would have to also approve.

That approval was finally announced on May 20, 2010. Zerwekh was ecstatic, only to have her excitement dashed once again in 2012 when Virginia Senator James Webb removed the provision for the Medal from the defense budget. The next year, the provision was placed back into the budget, and the Senate granted its approval as part of the budget vote. But the red tape was not finished. The nomination now had to be reviewed and approved by the Department of Defense. That approval was announced by White House officials on August 26, 2014.

On November 26, 2014, more than two dozen of the Cushing family's descendants gathered at the White House, where President Barack Obama presented Alonzo Cushing's Medal of Honor to Helen Bird Loring Ensign, Cushing's first cousin, twice removed, who accepted it on his behalf.

The citation presented with the Medal described Cushing's heroism on July 3, 1863:

> *First Lieutenant Alonzo H. Cushing distinguished himself by acts of bravery above and beyond the call of duty while serving as an artillery commander in Battery A, 4th U.S. Artillery, Army of the Potomac at Gettysburg, Pennsylvania on July 3rd, 1863 during the American Civil War. That morning, Confederate forces led by General Robert E. Lee began cannonading First Lieutenant Cushing's position on Cemetery Ridge. Using field glasses, First Lieutenant Cushing directed fire for his own artillery battery. He refused to leave the battlefield after being struck in the shoulder by a shell fragment. As he continued to direct fire, he was struck again—this time suffering grievous damage to his abdomen. Still refusing to abandon his command, he boldly stood tall in the face of Major General George E. Pickett's Charge and continued to direct devastating fire into oncoming forces. As the Confederate forces closed in, First Lieutenant Cushing was struck in*

the mouth by an enemy bullet and fell dead beside his gun. His gallant stand and fearless leadership inflicted severe casualties upon Confederate forces and opened wide gaps in their lines, directly impacting the Union force's ability to repel Pickett's Charge. First Lieutenant Cushing's extraordinary heroism and selflessness above and beyond the call of duty at the cost of his own life are in keeping with the highest traditions of military service and reflect great credit upon himself, Battery A, 4th U.S. Artillery, Army of the Potomac, and the United States Army.

With the presentation of Cushing's Medal, the last award for heroism in the Civil War had been issued.

Note: This section was adapted from one that originally appeared on the website of the Congressional Medal of Honor Society.

James B. Thompson, Sergeant, Company G, 1st Pennsylvania Rifles

James B. Thompson was born to John P. and Hannah (Gilson) Thompson on June 1, 1843. Some sources place his birth location as England, while others indicate it was Juniata County, Pennsylvania. Even his name is in question, as at least one source indicates that he also was known as George W. Bailey. The reason for this discrepancy in names is unknown. He will be referred to as James B. Thompson here.

Thompson mustered into the 13th Pennsylvania Reserves on June 8, 1861, as a sergeant in Company G. The 13th Pennsylvania Reserves would become known as the 42nd Pennsylvania Infantry. Not only was there a question of Thompson's name, but the 42nd Pennsylvania also had a rather convoluted history of name changes as well, beginning with the name Kane's Rifles, named for Colonel Thomas Kane, the regiment's organizer. Recruited in Elk County, Pennsylvania, Company G was also known as the Elk County Rifles. Each company was named for either the county in which the members were recruited or for an organizer, and collectively they became the 1st Pennsylvania Rifles. Every member of the regiment had to be a skilled marksman, and he had to wear the tail of a male deer in his hat as a means of identification, giving rise to the name Bucktails. Although unofficial, that name would stick with the regiment throughout the Civil War.

James B. Thompson. *Congressional Medal of Honor Society, Mount Pleasant, South Carolina.*

When the regiment reached Harrisburg for mustering in, the men learned that they would be organized as the 17th Regiment for three months' service. However, a 17th regiment had already been organized, and the 1st Pennsylvania Rifles was assigned to the Reserve Corps, a grouping of fifteen regiments that had been formed in excess of the number needed to meet Pennsylvania's designated quota. The 1st Rifles became the 13th Pennsylvania Reserves, and when the reserve regiments were re-designated, the 13th Pennsylvania Reserves became the 42nd Pennsylvania Infantry.

The regiment fought innumerous battles and skirmishes prior to Gettysburg and gained a well-earned reputation as being a formidable force. It arrived at Gettysburg on the second day of fighting, July 2, 1863, as part of the 1st Brigade, 3rd Division, 5th Corps. The men rested for a while, and then at about 4:00 p.m. they formed near Little Round Top, then moved to the Wheatfield, where Colonel Charles Taylor, commander of the regiment, was killed. Lieutenant Colonel Alanson E. Niles had already been wounded earlier, so command of the regiment fell to Major William Ross Hartshorn. As the Confederates gained control, the regiment fell back to the safety of a stone wall.

On July 3, the regiment moved in midafternoon from its position behind the wall into the Rose Woods beyond the Wheatfield. In the Rose Woods, the 15th Georgia Infantry had posted itself behind a temporary breastwork of rails on the right of the Confederate line. The Bucktails led a charge, with the rest of the brigade flowing close behind.

Under heavy fire, the regiment reached the Georgians, and fighting quickly became hand to hand. Thompson found himself engaged with the 15th Georgia's color bearer. Each grasping the flag's staff, Thompson and the color bearer punched, kicked and did anything they could to dislodge the other's hand. Finally, Thompson gained the upper hand, wresting the flag from its owner and taking the man captive. All around Thompson, other Georgians were surrendering as well. Those who didn't surrender began a chaotic retreat across the Jacob Weikert farm and toward Devil's Den. Some historians believe that it may be one of the men from the 15th Georgia, killed in the retreat, whose body was posed behind the famous Devil's Den barricade by photographer Alexander Gardner for his historic photo of a dead Confederate "sharpshooter."

Thompson marched his prisoner and the captured flag back to the Union line, where he learned that a significant part of the 15th Georgia had been taken captive.

Following the Battle of Gettysburg, Thompson remained with the regiment until he was captured at Bethesda Church on May 30, 1864. Exchanged the next day, he was transferred to the 190th Pennsylvania, where he eventually rose to the rank of captain. On March 13, 1865, he received a brevet promotion to major. He mustered out with his company June 28, 1865.

On December 1, 1864, Thompson was awarded the Medal of Honor for capturing the flag in the July 3 fighting. Without going into detail, his citation reads:

> *Capture of flag of 15th Georgia Infantry (C.S.A.).*

On August 31, 1875, Thompson died in Port Royal, Pennsylvania. He was buried at Port Royal's Old Churchill Cemetery.

HARVEY MAY MUNSELL, SERGEANT, COMPANY A, 99TH PENNSYLVANIA INFANTRY

From time to time, a man distinguishes himself continually, with no specific instance standing out among a history of heroic deeds. One such man was Harvey May Munsell.

Munsell was born on January 5, 1843, in Painted Post, New York. Tipping the scale at one hundred pounds, he left his job as manager of his uncle's lumberyard in Oil City, Pennsylvania, to enlist at the outset of the Civil War. His stature caused every enlistment station to turn him down until he found one in Philadelphia that would accept him. He enlisted in the 32nd Pennsylvania, which was renumbered the 99th Pennsylvania in February 1862. Despite his size, he was made color bearer.

In his first action during the Peninsula Campaign, he charged a line of Georgia troops while exhorting those behind him to follow. He was praised by his officers for being instrumental in halting the Confederate advance. At his next battle, at Chancellorsville, he and his unit were awarded the Kearny Cross for clearing a group of Confederates from a wooded area.

Harvey May Munsell. *Congressional Medal of Honor Society, Mount Pleasant, South Carolina.*

His third battle was at Gettysburg. Positioned at Devil's Den, the 99th Pennsylvania made several charges in which the entire color guard was either killed or wounded. Somehow, Munsell was uninjured. In the fight, an order was given to fall back. Munsell either did not hear the order or misunderstood. Before he could retreat, a shell burst near him, knocking him to the ground and into a crater that had been created by an earlier explosion. Stunned, he lay in the crater with his flag beneath him until his head cleared. The rest of the regiment, not seeing him when they regrouped, assumed that he had been killed or captured, along with the regiment's flag.

When Munsell peered over the top of the crater, he saw that he was so close to the Confederate line that any movement would expose him and the flag. His only hope was for the rest of the regiment to return or for the Rebels to move out of the area. Tucking the flag completely beneath him so that no part could be seen, he lay in the hole as if dead. His decision proved fortuitous because the 99th mounted a countercharge that took them right past him. Once they had gone through, Munsell rose up and joined in the assault.

Later, when after-battle reports were submitted, the commander of the 99th Pennsylvania, Major John W. Moore, noted that Munsell's actions were "worthy of the most decided approval." General J.H. Hobart Ward sent his own praises to Secretary of War Edwin Stanton.

Munsell took part in several additional battles after Gettysburg until he was given a furlough to attend the Free Military School in Washington, where he was promoted to first lieutenant. He then rejoined the 99th Pennsylvania and took part in additional action. At the Second Battle of Deep Bottom in August 1864, he was taken captive and held as a prisoner of war until he was released in 1865, whereupon he returned to his regiment yet again. Now a captain, he remained with the regiment until he was mustered out on July 1, 1865.

Less than a year later, on February 5, 1866, Munsell was awarded the Medal of Honor. The citation that accompanied the award read:

> *Gallant and courageous conduct as color bearer. (This noncommissioned officer carried the colors of his regiment through 13 engagements.)*

On February 9, 1913, Harvey Munsell passed away in Mount Vernon, New York. He was laid to rest at the Mount Auburn Cemetery in Cambridge, Massachusetts.

George Crawford Platt, Private, Troop H, 6th U.S. Cavalry

Martin Schwenk, Sergeant, Troop B, 6th U.S. Cavalry

When most people think about cavalry action at Gettysburg, if the thought comes to them at all, the East and South Cavalry Fields come to mind. A third action, often forgotten, took place that same day in Fairfield, a small village about eight miles southwest of Gettysburg. Although that skirmish was relatively small, it produced two Medal of Honor recipients. Both were foreign born.

George Crawford Platt was born on February 17, 1842, in Londonderry, Ireland, the son of Robert and Martha (Kilgil) Platt. About the time George was nine years old, the family came to the United States, settling in Philadelphia. On August 5, 1861, Platt enlisted as a private in the 3rd U.S. Cavalry. He was assigned to Troop H. Five days later, the regiment was re-designated as the 6th U.S. Cavalry, with the 3rd U.S. Cavalry designation assigned to the Regiment of Mounted Rifles.

Martin Schwenk was born in Baden, Germany, on April 28, 1839. Little is known of Schwenk's family or his younger years, other than that he was also known as George Martin. He will be referred to as Martin Schwenk in this work. When Schwenk signed on with the 6th U.S. Cavalry, he was assigned to Troop B.

Prior to coming to Fairfield, the 6th U.S. Cavalry participated in several skirmishes and battles, both large and small, including Chancellorsville, Brandy Station, Williamsburg and Yorktown. At Gettysburg (Fairfield), Major Samuel H. Starr was in command. The regiment carried the romantic nickname "Rush's Lancers," for Colonel Richard H. Rush, organizer of the regiment. It was the only cavalry unit in the army that carried lances, although the lances were abandoned after they were found to be impractical in forested areas.

Fairfield, also known as Millerstown, was no stranger to fighting. A raid by Brigadier General Albert Jenkins took place not far from town on June 21, 1863, and small skirmishes were fought on June 29–30.

On July 3, the 6th U.S. Cavalry moved at noon with the Cavalry Corps Reserve Brigade to attack the Confederate right and rear. However, when

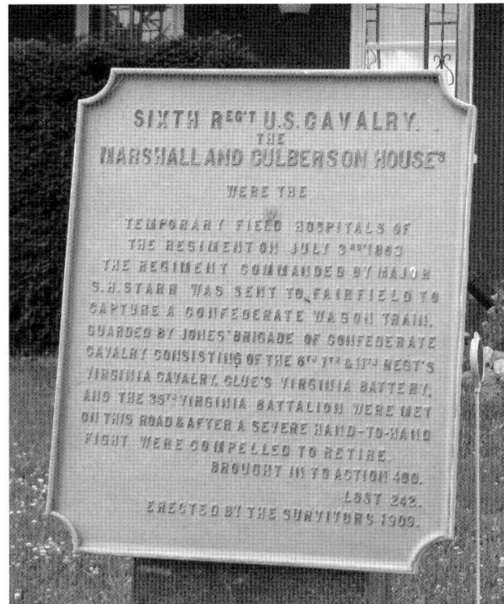

Left: George Crawford Platt. *Congressional Medal of Honor Society, Mount Pleasant, South Carolina.*

Right: This plaque in front of the J.A. Marshall farm, placed by the 6th U.S. Cavalry, commemorates the battle in which Martin Schwenk earned his Medal of Honor. *Author photo.*

word was received from a local civilian that a slow-moving Confederate wagon train was seen near Fairfield, Major Starr was directed to disengage and locate the wagons. The civilian was later suspected of being a Confederate sympathizer. Ordered to hold the town if he could capture the wagons, Starr knew that he would control access to Fairfield Gap and deprive the Confederates of the likely escape route Lee would take if pushed out of Gettysburg.

Arriving at Fairfield, he learned that the wagons had just passed through town and were headed in the direction of Cashtown. He formed three detachments from his four hundred men, with each going in a different direction in search of the train.

Before long, one of the units under Lieutenant Christian Balder encountered pickets of Brigadier General William E. "Grumble" Jones's 7th Virginia Cavalry but were forced to pull back when additional Confederate troops arrived. When his men returned and informed Starr that they had found Jones's troops, Starr took the 6th U.S. to a small ridge and set his men up on either side of the road.

When the 7th Virginia arrived, Starr's men pushed them back, inflicting such heavy casualties that the 7th Virginia was effectively out of the fight. With reinforcements from the 6th Virginia Cavalry, 11th Virginia Cavalry, 35th

Virginia Battalion and Captain Robert Chew's battery, the Rebels charged again, inflicting heavy losses on the outnumbered Union troops.

With the fight going badly, Schwenk was dispatched by Second Lieutenant Nicholas Nolan to go for assistance. Carrying the message, he tried to slash his way through the Confederate line but was driven back, unable to complete his mission. However, Nolan noted in his report that he personally observed Schwenk rescue an unknown officer who had been taken captive.

In the fight, the regiment's color bearer was killed. Seeing the man fall, several Confederates rushed forward in an attempt to capture the colors. Platt would have none of it, riding quickly between the colors and the Rebels. Using his saber, he fought off those intent on capturing the flag, grabbed the fallen colors and rode to safety. His action was credited with preventing the flag from falling into enemy hands.

Both sides fought viciously, using not only their guns but also their sabers. Other Union detachments from the 6th Cavalry arrived to help but were quickly overwhelmed. Balder was mortally wounded, and Starr was wounded so badly that his arm had to be amputated. Dozens of Federal troopers became prisoners. The Union line collapsed, with the men retreating toward the town of Fairfield.

Both Schwenk and Platt received Medals of Honor for the efforts, Schwenk on April 23, 1889, and Platt on July 12, 1895. Schwenk's citation noted his heroism by referring to his

> *Bravery in an attempt to carry a communication through the enemy's lines; also rescued an officer from the hands of the enemy.*

Platt's citation read:

> *Seized the regimental flag upon the death of the standard bearer in a hand-to-hand fight and prevented it from falling into the hands of the enemy.*

Platt died from endocarditis in Philadelphia on June 20, 1912, and was buried at Holy Cross Cemetery in Yeadon, Pennsylvania. Coincidentally, Schwenk died in Boston on that same date, but in 1924. He was buried at Arlington National Cemetery as George Martin.

Part VI

POST-BATTLE, JULY 1863

Charles Capehart, Major, 1st West Virginia Cavalry

Charles E. Capehart was born in 1833 just outside Johnstown, Pennsylvania, the younger of two Capehart brothers. After their mother died when the brothers were young, Charles, his father and his brother, Henry, moved to Pittsburgh. Both brothers attended schools in that city.

When the Civil War began, Charles was living in Du Quoin, Illinois. On April 18, 1861, he enlisted in the Union army, officially mustering in on May 2. He served for three months in Company G of the 12th Illinois Infantry before having to muster out due to illness. Six weeks later, he reenlisted, this time as the adjutant for the 31st Illinois Infantry, serving until May 16, 1862, when he was commissioned as a captain and assigned to the 1st Virginia Cavalry (Union). His regiment would change its name to the 1st West Virginia Cavalry when West Virginia became a state in 1863. On June 6, 1863, he was promoted to major, less than a month before the Battle of Gettysburg. Meanwhile, Henry also enlisted and was serving with his brother in the 1st West Virginia Cavalry as the regimental surgeon.

At Gettysburg on July 3, 1863, Charles helped lead a charge against firmly entrenched Confederate troops. The charge resulted in severe casualties for the West Virginians, as well as brigade commander General Elon Farnsworth, who was killed. With Farnsworth's death, Colonel Nathaniel P. Richmond, who had been commanding the 1st West Virginia Cavalry, was moved into Farnsworth's position as commander of the brigade. Charles

Capehart moved into Richmond's old position and took command of the regiment. Details of this charge are described in Part V in the accounting of William Wells's story.

Charles E. Capehart. *Congressional Medal of Honor Society, Mount Pleasant, South Carolina.*

On the evening of July 4, with Lee's army now in full retreat, a civilian who had learned of the army moving through Monterey Pass mounted his horse and traveled toward Emmitsburg, hoping to encounter Union troops. When he encountered a scout from General George Custer's Brigade, he reported what he had seen at Monterey Pass. The scout, in turn, made his way back to General Custer at Emmitsburg to report the information.

The oppressive heat that marked the fighting at Gettysburg the previous three days gave way to a driving rainstorm as Custer's Brigade was dispatched toward the mountain. There, he was ambushed by artillery and hidden Confederate troops, and a fierce battle ensued. The fighting raged for several hours in the darkness, where both sides depended on the brightness of lightning flashes to determine the locations of the opposing troops.

Capehart and the 1st West Virginia Cavalry arrived at the fight at the peak of the chaos, with panicked horses stampeding through both battle lines. The rainstorm had blotted out any light from the moon, and smoke from the battle made it nearly impossible to see. Fearing his men could be shot by either side in the darkness, or even by their own comrades, Capehart ordered his troopers to draw their sabers so they would be able to identify one another. Just as Custer's horse was shot, Capehart ordered his men to charge into the fray.

The men of the 1st West Virginia Cavalry followed Capehart in the dash down the side of the mountain into the Confederate line. Surprised by the daring charge, many Southerners began retreating in total disarray. The rest began hand-to-hand fighting in the darkness. Little by little, the West Virginians began taking prisoners and destroying wagons. By the time the fighting ended, Capehart and his men had captured or destroyed three hundred wagons and fifteen ambulances and captured 1,300 prisoners, 200 of them commissioned officers, as well as a large number of horses and mules.

On August 1, 1864, Charles was promoted to lieutenant colonel, and following Lee's surrender at Appomattox in 1865, Capehart mustered out of the Union army. On April 7, 1898, just three years after his brother, Henry, was awarded the Medal of Honor for saving a drowning soldier while under fire, Charles was awarded one of his own. In addition to the Capehart brothers, twelve members of the 1st West Virginia Cavalry received Medals of Honor for their actions during the Civil War.

Charles's citation read:

> *While commanding the regiment, Major Capehart charged down the mountain side at midnight, in a heavy rain, upon the enemy's fleeing wagon train. Many wagons were captured and destroyed and many prisoners taken.*

Charles Capehart died on July 11, 1911, in Washington, D.C., and is buried in Section 3 of Arlington National Cemetery.

Note: This section was adapted from one that originally appeared on the website of the Congressional Medal of Honor Society.

Charles Maynard (Myron) Holton, First Sergeant, Company A, 7th Michigan Cavalry

Charles M. Holton, born in Potter, New York, on May 25, 1839, had the distinction of being the last man to earn the Medal of Honor in the Gettysburg Campaign. Holton, whose middle name was either Maynard or Myron, depending on the source, was also the last man to capture a Confederate flag in the campaign.

Although there were rumblings that certain Southern states might secede from the Union, it was still only angry talk in 1860 when the twenty-two-year-old Holton moved from New York to Battle Creek, Michigan. His reason for the move was to join his brother, Samuel, who had moved to Battle Creek earlier and was practicing medicine there. Once in Battle Creek, Charles earned his law degree and began practicing law.

When the Civil War began, Holton enlisted as a sergeant in Company A of the 7th Michigan Cavalry, part of the Michigan Brigade, made up of the 1st, 5th, 6th and 7th Michigan Cavalries. Initially, the 7th Michigan Cavalry was commanded by its organizer, Colonel William Mann, a prominent newspaper publisher in Michigan. Just a few days before arriving at Gettysburg, the brigade was placed under a newly minted Brigadier General George Armstrong Custer.

Charles M. Holton. *Congressional Medal of Honor Society, Mount Pleasant, South Carolina.*

At Gettysburg, the 7th Michigan Cavalry took part in Custer's famous charge at the East Cavalry Field on July 3. When Robert E. Lee began his retreat back to Virginia following the battle, the brigade was part of the following Union army, taking part in a number of skirmishes along the way with Lee's rear guard.

On the morning of July 14, 1863, that rear guard was defending a pontoon bridge crossing at Falling Waters, Virginia. For some reason, the Confederates had not set out any pickets, and as they ate breakfast while waiting to cross the river, they were surprised by two companies from the 6th Michigan Cavalry.

In the ensuing battle, the 1st Battalion of the 7th Michigan Cavalry, consisting of only seventy sabers, formed into a column of fours and charged into the main body of Confederates. Facing a flurry of bullets, they slashed their way through the ranks. In doing so, Holton saw the color bearer of the 55th Virginia Infantry fall wounded. Dismounting his horse, Holton rushed to the wounded man, seizing his colors. Rushing back to his horse, Holton reported hearing the man shout out, "You Yanks have been after that flag for a long time but you never got it till now."

Holton remounted and returned to the regiment, which was preparing for another charge. At that point, the Confederates threw down their arms, with nearly five hundred of them being taken captive.

When the captured flag was examined, it showed all the battles where the 55th Virginia had fought, including Gaines' Mill, Frayser's Farm, Cedar Mountain, Second Bull Run, the Siege of Harpers Ferry, Antietam, Fredericksburg and Chancellorsville, in addition to numerous smaller engagements and skirmishes. The flag was eventually returned to Virginia, and it rests today in the Museum of the Confederacy.

By the time of his discharge, Holton had attained the rank of second lieutenant. Returning to civilian life, he married Mary Thisler in 1864.

On March 21, 1889, he was awarded with the Medal of Honor, with a citation that read:

> *Capture of flag of 55th Virginia Infantry (C.S.A.). In the midst of the battle with foot soldiers he dismounted to capture the flag.*

Charles Holton died in Yakima, Washington, on August 25, 1899. His remains were returned to Battle Creek, Michigan, for burial at Oak Hill Cemetery.

Appendix A

WHY MEDALS OF HONOR WERE AWARDED FOR CAPTURING A FLAG

Readers have likely noticed that a large number of the Medals of Honor were awarded for capturing a flag. In fact, of the seventy-two Medals awarded at Gettysburg, twenty-five were for capturing a flag. Several other flags were captured in which no Medal was awarded. Further, an additional seven Medals were awarded for saving a regiment's own flag. What was it about capturing an enemy's flag, or saving one's own, that justified so many awards?

It is important to note that the Civil War still followed the Napoleonic tradition in which soldiers stood side by side in a long line, firing or moving in unison. It didn't take long for the battlefield to be enveloped in a heavy cover of gun smoke, making it virtually impossible for a soldier to see more than a few feet to either side. This lack of visibility caused confusion and made it difficult for officers to control the line.

The use of battle flags was quickly adopted by both sides as a means of providing a visual point of reference for the regiment. Flags provided a personal connection to home for the men. Presented to the regiment just before it marched off to war, the flags often were handmade by the women of the town from which the regiment was formed. This personal touch instilled a reminder of what, and who, the men were fighting for. Whether Union or Confederate, the regimental flag provided a tangible symbol of home.

The color bearer was placed near the center of the line, usually a few paces in front of the formation, and every soldier on both sides knew the importance of knowing where the flag was at all times. Each man used the color bearer's position as his own, moving forward or back and maintaining order, depending on what the color bearer did. The color bearer also dictated the cadence, or speed, at which the line advanced. Without the color bearer, chaos took over.

The color bearer himself normally did not carry a weapon. Therefore, to protect the flag, a color guard was positioned on either side of the color bearer with orders to protect the flag with their lives. The color guard consisted of two to nine men who were selected for their bravery and coolness under fire.

Both sides recognized very early in the war that if they could kill the color bearer, or at least capture his flag, the enemy's battle line would be plunged into disarray and placed at a tremendous disadvantage.

It took a brave man to carry the colors, and few of them made it through the entire war unscathed. Despite the danger, every man, particularly those in the color guard, knew it was his duty to immediately pick up the flag when the color bearer was struck down, carrying it until he himself was wounded or killed. As a result, it was not uncommon in large battles for a regiment or company to lose multiple color bearers over the course of the fight. Conversely, those who tried to capture a flag also often paid with their lives.

Protecting the colors was so important that, when it saw it was about to be overrun, the 16th Maine Infantry, fighting on Oak Ridge on the first day of fighting at Gettysburg, actually tore its regimental flag into tiny pieces and gave a piece to each man to hide on his body. Even though it could no longer serve its original purpose, this ensured that it would not be captured.

Appendix B

CRITERIA FOR EARNING THE MEDAL OF HONOR

The Medal of Honor is the highest award bestowed on American military personnel. There are three distinct versions of the Medal: one for the U.S. Army, one for the U.S. Air Force and one that is used for the U.S. Navy, Marine Corps and U.S. Coast Guard.

On January 29, 1963, House Resolution no. 2998 was introduced by Congressman Philip Joseph Philbin from Massachusetts to establish standards for the awarding of certain medals to members of the armed services, including the Medal of Honor. The House Armed Services Committee discussed the resolution and reported back to the House of Representatives on June 18, 1963. The resolution passed in the House on July 8. The Senate Armed Services Committee then considered the resolution and reported to the full Senate on July 16; the Senate approved it the same day. With both the House and Senate in agreement, the resolution was sent to President John Fitzgerald Kennedy, who signed it into law.

The law authorizes the award to be presented by the president of the United States on behalf of Congress to members of the United States Armed Forces who show conspicuous gallantry while risking their lives in a manner that is above and beyond the call of duty under the following conditions:

- *While engaged in an action against an enemy of the United States*
- *While engaged in military operations involving conflict with an opposing foreign force; or*

- *While serving with friendly forces engaged in an armed conflict against an opposing armed force in which the United States is not a belligerent party*

All recommendations for the award must include a thorough report on the action taken by the individual, the battle in which that action took place and the setting. It must also include at least two sworn eyewitness statement, as well as any other supporting or compelling evidence that can be obtained.

The recommendation must then be approved up through the military chain of command, ending with the president of the United States as commander in chief.

The statute further requires that recommendations for the Medal must be submitted within three years of the action, and the Medal must be presented within five years. An Act of Congress is required to waive these time limits for any submission that falls outside this timeline. It was this clause that was invoked to allow the Medal presentation to First Lieutenant Alonzo Cushing on November 26, 2014, for his heroic actions at Gettysburg on July 3, 1863 (see Part V).

Appendix C

MEDALS OF HONOR AWARDED BY STATE IN THE GETTYSBURG CAMPAIGN

State	**Pre-Battle**	**Battle Day 1**	**Battle Day 2**	**Battle Day 3**	**Post-Battle**	**Total**
Pennsylvania		5	11	4		**20**
New York	3	1	3	6		**13**
Massachusetts			2	5		**7**
Ohio	2		2	2		**6**
Vermont			1	3		**4**
Delaware			1	2		**3**
Connecticut				3		**3**
Maine			2			**2**
Minnesota				2		**2**
Wisconsin		2				**2**
West Virginia	1				1	**2**
Indiana				1		**1**
Michigan					1	**1**
U.S. Regulars			1	5		**6**
Total	**6**	**8**	**23**	**33**	**2**	**72**

WORKS CITED

Part I

American Battlefield Trust. "Designing the Medal of Honor." https://www.battlefields.org/learn/articles/designing-medal-honor. Accessed July 29, 2022.

Congressional Medal of Honor Society. "Medal of Honor History & Timeline: A History of Heroism." https://www.cmohs.org/medal/timeline. Accessed July 29, 2022.

———. "Related Medal of Honor Recipients." https://www.cmohs.org/recipients/lists/related-recipients. Accessed July 30, 2022.

New World Encyclopedia. "Medal of Honor." https://www.newworldencyclopedia.org/entry/Medal_of_Honor. Accessed July 29, 2022.

Nye, Logan. "The Unknown Deceased Who Have Received the Medal of Honor." We Are the Mighty. https://www.wearethemighty.com/mighty-history/unknown-soldier-medal-of-honor. Accessed August 1, 2022.

Wikipedia. "Frocking." https://en.wikipedia.org/wiki/Frocking. Accessed July 29, 2022.

Part II

James Robinson Durham

Congressional Medal of Honor Society. "James Robinson Durham." https://www.cmohs.org/recipients/james-r-durham. Accessed July 28, 2022.

Emerging Civil War. "Three Medals of Honor and the Second Battle of Winchester." https://emergingcivilwar.com/2019/06/15/three-medals-of-honor-and-the-second-battle-of-winchester. Accessed July 29, 2022.

Find A Grave. "James Robinson Durham." https://www.findagrave.com/memorial/6172407/james-robinson-durham. Accessed July 28, 2022.

National Park Service. "Second Battle of Winchester." https://www.nps.gov/cebe/learn/historyculture/second-battle-of-winchester.htm. Accessed August 5, 2022.

John Thomas Patterson

American Civil War. "Medal of Honor." https://americancivilwar.com/medal_of_honor7.html. Accessed August 5, 2022.

Congressional Medal of Honor Society. "John Thomas Patterson." https://www.cmohs.org/recipients/john-t-patterson. Accessed August 5, 2022.

Emerging Civil War. "Three Medals of Honor and the Second Battle of Winchester." https://emergingcivilwar.com/2019/06/15/three-medals-of-honor-and-the-second-battle-of-winchester. Accessed July 29, 2022.

Find A Grave. "John T. Patterson." https://www.findagrave.com/memorial/7932002/john-t-patterson. Accessed August 5, 2022.

National Park Service. "Second Battle of Winchester." https://www.nps.gov/cebe/learn/historyculture/second-battle-of-winchester.htm. Accessed August 5, 2022.

Wikipedia. "122nd Ohio Infantry Regiment." https://en.wikipedia.org/wiki/122nd_Ohio_Infantry_Regiment. Accessed August 5, 2022.

Elbridge Robinson

American Civil War. "Medal of Honor." https://americancivilwar.com/medal_of_honor2.html. Accessed July 29, 2022.

Congressional Medal of Honor Society. "Elbridge Robinson." https://www.cmohs.org/recipients/elbridge-robinson. Accessed July 29, 2022.

Emerging Civil War. "Three Medals of Honor and the Second Battle of Winchester." https://emergingcivilwar.com/2019/06/15/three-medals-of-honor-and-the-second-battle-of-winchester. Accessed July 29, 2022.

Marion County, Illinois. https://marioncountyil.angelfire.com/iVernonIllinois.html.

Nathan Mullock Hallock

Congressional Medal of Honor Society. "Nathan Hallock." https://www.cmohs.org/recipients/nathan-m-hallock. Accessed August 1, 2022.

Find A Grave. "Nathan Hallock." https://www.findagrave.com/memorial/7242135/nathan-mullock-hallock. Accessed August 3, 2022.

Horrigan, Jeremiah. "Medal of Honor Winners Went Far Beyond Call of Duty in Serving Our Nation." *Middletown (NY) Times Herald-Record*, May 28, 2012.

New York State Military Museum. "Muster-In Roll, Field and Staff, 124th Regiment, NYSV," page 415. https://museum.dmna.ny.gov/unit-history/conflict/us-civil-war-1861-1865/civil-war-muster-rolls/infantry-regiments. Accessed August 4, 2022.

Wikipedia. "Nathan M. Hallock." https://en.wikipedia.org/wiki/Nathan_M._Hallock. Accessed August 1, 2022.

Luigi Palma di Cesnola

American Battlefield Trust. "Aldie." https://www.battlefields.org/learn/civil-war/battles/aldie. Accessed August 6, 2022.

American Civil War. "Medal of Honor." https://americancivilwar.com/medal_of_honor2.html. Accessed August 6, 2022.

Congressional Medal of Honor Society. "Louis Palma di Cesnola." https://www.cmohs.org/recipients/louis-p-di-cesnola. Accessed August 5, 2022.

Phisterer, Frederick. *New York in the War of the Rebellion*. 3rd ed. Albany, NY: J.B. Lyon Company, 1912.

Wikipedia. "Luigi Palma di Cesnola." https://en.wikipedia.org/wiki/Luigi_Palma_di_Cesnola. Accessed August 6, 2022.

Thomas M. Burke

American Civil War. "Medal of Honor." https://americancivilwar.com/medal_of_honor1.html. Accessed August 3, 2022.

Boatner, Mark M. *The Civil War Dictionary*. New York: Vintage Books, 1991.

Congressional Medal of Honor Society. "Thomas M. Burke." https://www.cmohs.org/recipients/thomas-m-burke. Accessed August 3, 2022.

Gindlesperger, James. *Bullets and Bandages*. Durham, NC: Blair, 2020.

Historical Marker Database. https://www.hmdb.org/m.asp?m=197243. Accessed August 4, 2022.

Part III

Jefferson Coates

American Civil War. "Medal of Honor." https://americancivilwar.com/medal_of_honor2.html. Accessed July 29, 2022.

Congressional Medal of Honor Society. "Jefferson Coates." https://www.cmohs.org/recipients/jefferson-coates. Accessed August 1, 2022.

Find A Grave. "Jefferson Coates." https://www.findagrave.com/memorial/19733/jefferson-coates. Accessed July 30, 2022.

Wikipedia. "Jefferson Coates." https://en.wikipedia.org/wiki/Jefferson_Coates. Accessed July 30, 2022.

———. "7th Wisconsin Infantry Regiment." https://en.wikipedia.org/wiki/7th_Wisconsin_Infantry_Regiment. Accessed July 30, 2022.

Wisconsin Historical Society. "Jefferson Coates." https://www.wisconsinhistory.org/Records/Image/IM3898. Accessed July 30, 2022.

Edward Lyons Gilligan

American Civil War. "Medal of Honor." https://americancivilwar.com/medal_of_honor3.html. Accessed August 8, 2022.

Congressional Medal of Honor Society. "Edward Lyons Gilligan." https://www.cmohs.org/recipients/edward-l-gilligan. Accessed August 7, 2022.

Pennsylvania in the Civil War. "Muster Roll, 88th Regiment Pennsylvania Volunteers, Company E." https://www.pa-roots.com/pacw/infantry/88th/88thcoe.html. Accessed August 7, 2022.

Wikipedia. "88th Pennsylvania Infantry Regiment." https://en.wikipedia.org/wiki/88th_Pennsylvania_Infantry_Regiment. Accessed August 8, 2022.

WikiTree. "Edward Lyons Gilligan." https://www.wikitree.com/wiki/Gilligan-111. Accessed August 8, 2022.

Henry Shippen Huidekoper

American Civil War. "Medal of Honor." https://americancivilwar.com/medal_of_honor4.html. Accessed August 9, 2022.

Congressional Medal of Honor Society. "Henry Shippen Huidekoper." https://www.cmohs.org/recipients/henry-s-huidekoper. Accessed August 9, 2022.

Gindlesperger, James. *Bullets and Bandages*. Durham, NC: Blair, 2020.

Huidekoper, Henry S., and G.W. Jones. "Official Reports for the 150th Pennsylvania Numbers 67 and 68." *Official Records*, series 1, vol. 27, part 1. Washington, D.C.: U.S. Government Printing Office, 1880–1901, 346–58.

Wikipedia. "Henry S. Huidekoper." https://en.wikipedia.org/wiki/Henry_S._Huidekoper. Accessed August 9, 2022.

———. "150th Pennsylvania Infantry Regiment." https://en.wikipedia.org/wiki/150th_Pennsylvania_Infantry_Regiment. Accessed August 9, 2022.

Francis Irsch

American Civil War. "Medal of Honor." https://americancivilwar.com/medal_of_honor4.html. Accessed August 9, 2022.

Congressional Medal of Honor Society. "Francis Irsch." https://www.cmohs.org/recipients/francis-irsch. Accessed August 9, 2022.

Find A Grave. "Francis Irsch." https://www.findagrave.com/memorial/7135667/francis-irsch. Accessed August 9, 2022.

Gindlesperger, James. *Escape from Libby Prison*. Shippensburg, PA: Burd Street Press, 1996.

James Monroe Reisinger

American Civil War. "Medal of Honor." https://americancivilwar.com/medal_of_honor7.html. Accessed August 9, 2022.

Chamberlain, Thomas. *History of the 150th Regiment Pennsylvania Volunteers, Second Regiment, Bucktail Brigade*. Baltimore, MD: Butternut and Blue, April 1, 1986.

Congressional Medal of Honor Society. "James Monroe Reisinger." https://www.cmohs.org/recipients/james-m-reisinger. Accessed August 9, 2022.

Military Images Digital. "Three Bullets at Gettysburg." https://www.militaryimagesmagazine-digital.com/2017/06/03/the-honored-few-summer-2017. Accessed August 9, 2022.

James May Rutter

American Civil War. "Medal of Honor." https://americancivilwar.com/medal_of_honor7.html. Accessed August 9, 2022.

Beyer, W.F., and G.F. Keydel, eds. *Deeds of Valor*. Detroit, MI: Perrien-Keydel Company, 1903.

Congressional Medal of Honor Society. "James May Rutter." https://www.cmohs.org/recipients/james-m-rutter. Accessed August 9, 2022.

Pennsylvania in the Civil War. "Infantry Regiments, 143rd Infantry, Company C." https://www.pa-roots.com/pacw/infantry/paregimentsnew3.html. Accessed August 9, 2022.

Alfred Jacob Sellers

American Civil War. "Medal of Honor." https://americancivilwar.com/medal_of_honor8.html. Accessed August 9, 2022.

Antietam on the Web. https://antietam.aotw.org/moh.php?citation_id=64. Accessed August 10, 2022.

Congressional Medal of Honor Society. "Alfred Jacob Sellers." https://www.cmohs.org/recipients/alfred-j-sellers Accessed August 10, 2022.

Student of the American Civil War. "The 90th Pennsylvania on July 1, 1863." https://studycivilwar.wordpress.com/2013/01/15/the-90th-pennsylvania-on-july-1-1863. Accessed August 10, 2022.

Wikipedia. "Alfred J. Sellers." https://en.wikipedia.org/wiki/Alfred_J._Sellers. Accessed August 10, 2022.

Francis Ashbury Waller

American Civil War. "Medal of Honor." https://americancivilwar.com/medal_of_honor8.html. Accessed August 9, 2022.

Beaudot, William J.K., and Lance J. Herdegen. *Into the Bloody Railroad Cut at Gettysburg*. Reprint ed. El Dorado Hills, CA: Savas Beatie, 2016.

Congressional Medal of Honor Society. "Francis A. Waller." https://www.cmohs.org/recipients/francis-a-waller. Accessed August 10, 2022.

Dawes, Lieutenant Colonel R.R. "Official Reports of Lieutenant-Colonel Rufus R. Dawes, 6th Wisconsin Infantry, No. 35." *Official Records*, series 1, vol. 27, part 1, no. 33. Washington, D.C.: U.S. Government Printing Office, 1880–1901, 275–78.

(Eau Claire, WI) *Leader-Telegram*. "Stolen Medal Recovered 14 Years Later." March 3, 1991, 20.s

Milwaukee Sunday Telegraph. Interview with Samuel Waller, July 29, 1883.

State of Wisconsin. *Roster of Wisconsin Volunteers—War of the Rebellion, 1861–1865*. Vol. 50. Madison, WI: Democrat Printing Company, State Printers, 1886.

Wikipedia. "Francis A. Wallar." https://en.wikipedia.org/wiki/Francis_A._Wallar. Accessed August 10, 2022.

Part IV

Nathaniel M. Allen

American Civil War. "Medal of Honor." https://americancivilwar.com/medal_of_honor1.html. Accessed August 9, 2022.

Browne, Patrick. "1st Massachusetts Infantry at Gettysburg." Historical Digression. https://historicaldigression.com/2012/12/29/1st-massachusetts-infantry-at-gettysburg. Accessed August 10, 2022.

Congressional Medal of Honor Society. "Nathaniel M. Allen." https://www.cmohs.org/recipients/nathaniel-m-allen. Accessed August 10, 2022.

Wikipedia. "Nathaniel M. Allen." https://en.wikipedia.org/wiki/Nathaniel_M._Allen. Accessed August 10, 2022.

John Barclay Fassett

American Civil War. "Medal of Honor." https://americancivilwar.com/medal_of_honor1.html. Accessed August 9, 2022.

Beyer, W.F., and G.F. Keydel, eds. *Deeds of Valor*. Detroit, MI: Perrien-Keydel Company, 1903.

Congressional Medal of Honor Society. "John Barclay Fassett." https://www.cmohs.org/recipients/john-b-fassett. Accessed August 10, 2022.

Find A Grave. "John Barclay Fassett." https://www.findagrave.com/memorial/23411/john-barclay-fassitt. Accessed August 10, 2022.

"History of the Twenty-Third Pennsylvania Volunteer Infantry, Birney's Zouaves: Three Months and Three Years Service, Civil War." Penn State University Library Digital Collections. https://digital.libraries.psu.edu/digital/collection/digitalbks2/id/80638, 288. Accessed August 10, 2022.

23d Regiment Pennsylvania Volunteers, Company F. https://www.pa-roots.com/pacw/infantry/23rd/23dcof3yrs.html. Accessed August 10, 2022.

Charles Stacey

American Civil War. "Medal of Honor." https://americancivilwar.com/medal_of_honor8.html. Accessed August 11, 2022.

Ancestry. "Charles Stacey and the Medal of Honor." Medic in the Green Time. http://medicinthegreentime.com/wp-content/uploads/2014/08/CHARLES-STACEY-ACCOUNT-OF-MOG.pdf. Accessed August 11, 2022.

Congressional Medal of Honor Society. "Charles Stacey." https://www.cmohs.org/recipients/charles-stacey. Accessed August 11, 2022.

Military Wiki. "Charles Stacey (Medal of Honor)." https://military-history.fandom.com/wiki/Charles_Stacey_(Medal_of_Honor). Accessed August 11, 2022.

Wikipedia. "Charles Stacey." https://en.wikipedia.org/wiki/Charles_Stacey_(Medal_of_Honor). Accessed August 11, 2022.

Mears et al.

American Civil War. "Medal of Honor." https://americancivilwar.com/medal_of_honor6.html. Accessed August 9, 2022.

Bates, Samuel P. (Samuel Penniman). *History of the Pennsylvania Volunteers, 1861–65*. Vol. 1. Harrisburg, PA: B. Singerly, State Printer, 1869–71.
Congressional Medal of Honor Society. "Chester S. Furman." https://www.cmohs.org/recipients/chester-s-furman. Accessed August 11, 2022.
———. "George W. Mears." https://www.cmohs.org/recipients/george-w-mears. Accessed August 11, 2022.
———. "James L. Roush." https://www.cmohs.org/recipients/james-l-roush. Accessed August 11, 2022.
———. "John W. Hart." https://www.cmohs.org/recipients/john-w-hart. Accessed August 11, 2022.
———. "Thaddeus S. Smith." https://www.cmohs.org/recipients/thaddeus-s-smith. Accessed August 11, 2022.
———. "Wallace W. Johnson." https://www.cmohs.org/recipients/wallace-w-johnson. Accessed August 11, 2022.
Wikipedia. "George Mears." https://en.wikipedia.org/wiki/George_Mears. Accessed August 11, 2022.

Thomas Horan

American Civil War. "Medal of Honor." https://americancivilwar.com/medal_of_honor4.html. Accessed August 11, 2022.
Barram, Rick. *The 72nd New York Infantry in the Civil War: A History and Roster.* Jefferson, NC: McFarland, 2014.
The Civil War in the East. "72nd New York Infantry Regiment." https://civilwarintheeast.com/us-regiments-batteries/new-york-infantry/72nd-new-york. Accessed August 11, 2022.
Congressional Medal of Honor Society. "Thomas Horan." https://www.cmohs.org/recipients/thomas-horan. Accessed August 11, 2022.
New York State Military Museum and Veterans Research Center. "72nd New York Infantry Regiment." https://museum.dmna.ny.gov/unit-history/infantry-1/72nd-infantry-regiment. Accessed August 11, 2022.
Wikipedia. "Thomas Horan." https://en.wikipedia.org/wiki/Thomas_Horan_(Medal_of_Honor). Accessed August 11, 2022.

Richard Enderlin

American Civil War. "Medal of Honor." https://americancivilwar.com/medal_of_honor3.html. Accessed July 8, 2022.

Congressional Medal of Honor Society. "Richard Enderlin." https://www.cmohs.org/recipients/richard-enderlin. Accessed August 6, 2022.

Hurst, Samuel H. *Journal-History of the Seventy-Third Ohio Volunteer Infantry*. Chillicothe, OH: 1866.

Lange, Katie. "U.S. Department of Defense, Medal of Honor Monday: Army Sgt. Richard Enderlin." *DOD News*, July 6, 2020.

Lankard, Joseph R. "Nixon's Gettysburg: 20 Years in the Secret Service." Rufus Youngblood blog. https://www.rufusyoungblood.com/blog/nixons-gettysburg. Accessed July 6, 2022.

Wikipedia. "Richard Enderlin." https://en.wikipedia.org/wiki/Richard_Enderlin. Accessed August 5, 2022.

Joshua Chamberlain

American Battlefield Trust. "Defense of Little Round Top." https://www.battlefields.org/learn/articles/defense-little-round-top. Accessed August 11, 2022.

American Civil War. "Medal of Honor." https://americancivilwar.com/medal_of_honor2.html. Accessed August 11, 2022.

The Battle of Gettysburg. "20th Maine Volunteer Infantry Regiment." https://gettysburg.stonesentinels.com/union-monuments/maine/20th-maine. Accessed August 11, 2022.

Congressional Medal of Honor Society. "Joshua L. Chamberlain." https://www.cmohs.org/recipients/joshua-l-chamberlain. Accessed August 11, 2022.

Wikipedia. "Joshua Chamberlain." https://en.wikipedia.org/wiki/Joshua_Chamberlain. Accessed August 11, 2022.

Andrew Jackson Tozier

American Battlefield Trust. "Defense of Little Round Top." https://www.battlefields.org/learn/articles/defense-little-round-top. Accessed August 11, 2022.

American Civil War. "Medal of Honor." https://americancivilwar.com/medal_of_honor8.html. Accessed August 11, 2022.

Congressional Medal of Honor Society. "Andrew J. Tozier." https://www.cmohs.org/recipients/andrew-j-tozier. Accessed August 11, 2022.

Emerging Civil War. "Recruiting the Regiment: The 2nd Maine Volunteer Infantry." https://emergingcivilwar.com/2021/06/04/recruiting-the-regiment-the-2nd-maine-volunteer-infantry. Accessed August 11, 2022.

Wikipedia. "Andrew J. Tozier." https://en.wikipedia.org/wiki/Andrew_J._Tozier. Accessed August 11, 2022.

Edward M. Knox

American Civil War. "Medal of Honor." https://americancivilwar.com/medal_of_honor4.html. Accessed August 11, 2022.

The Battle of Gettysburg. "15th New York Independent Battery." https://gettysburg.stonesentinels.com/union-monuments/new-york/new-york-artillery-and-engineers/15th-new-york-independent-battery. Accessed August 11, 2022.

Congressional Medal of Honor Society. "Edward M. Knox." https://www.cmohs.org/recipients/edward-m-knox. Accessed August 11, 2022.

Wikipedia. "Edward M. Knox." https://en.wikipedia.org/wiki/Edward_M._Knox. Accessed August 11, 2022.

Harrison Clark

American Civil War. "Medal of Honor." https://americancivilwar.com/medal_of_honor2.html. Accessed August 11, 2022.

Congressional Medal of Honor Society. "Harrison Clark." https://www.cmohs.org/recipients/harrison-clark. Accessed August 11, 2022.

Department of New York. "Sons of Union Veterans of the Civil War, Harrison Clark." https://nysuvcw.org/history/ny-gar-commanders/harrison-clark. Accessed August 11, 2022.

Find A Grave. "Harrison Clark." https://www.findagrave.com/memorial/19736/harrison-clark. Accessed August 11, 2022.

Hall of Valor Project. "Harrison Clark." https://valor.militarytimes.com/hero/1213. Accessed August 11, 2022.

Haskell, Lieutenant Harry L. "Report of Lieutenant Harry L. Haskell, 125th New York Infantry, No. 131." *Official Records*, series 1, vol. 27, part 1. Washington, D.C.: U.S. Government Printing Office, 1880–1901.

Wikipedia. "125th New York Infantry Regiment." https://en.wikipedia.org/wiki/125th_New_York_Infantry_Regiment. Accessed August 11, 2022.

Wikiwand. "Harrison Clark." https://www.wikiwand.com/en/Harrison_Clark. Accessed August 11, 2022.

Casper R. Carlisle

American Civil War. "Medal of Honor." https://americancivilwar.com/medal_of_honor2.html. Accessed August 12, 2022.

The Battle of Gettysburg. "Pennsylvania Independent Batteries C & F." https://gettysburg.stonesentinels.com/union-monuments/pennsylvania/pennsylvania-artillery/pennsylvania-independent-batteries-c-f. Accessed August 12, 2022.

Clark, William. *History of Hampton Battery F.* Akron, OH: Werner Company, 1909.

Congressional Medal of Honor Society. "Casper R. Carlisle." https://www.cmohs.org/recipients/casper-r-carlisle. Accessed August 12, 2022.

Charles Wellington Reed

American Civil War. "Medal of Honor." https://americancivilwar.com/medal_of_honor7.html. Accessed August 13, 2022.

The Battle of Gettysburg. "9th Massachusetts Battery." https://gettysburg.stonesentinels.com/union-monuments/massachusetts/9th-massachusetts-battery. Accessed August 13, 2022.

Congressional Medal of Honor Society. "Charles W. Reed." https://www.cmohs.org/recipients/charles-w-reed. Accessed August 13, 2022.

The Petersburg Project. "Artist Charles Wellington Reed at Petersburg." http://www.petersburgproject.org/charles-wellington-reed.html. Accessed August 13, 2022.

Wikipedia. "Charles W. Reed." https://en.wikipedia.org/wiki/Charles_W._Reed. Accessed August 13, 2022.

———. "9th Massachusetts Battery." https://en.wikipedia.org/wiki/9th_Massachusetts_Battery. Accessed August 13, 2022.

James Jackson Purman

American Civil War. "Medal of Honor." https://americancivilwar.com/medal_of_honor5.html. Accessed August 13, 2022.

Bates, Samuel P. (Samuel Penniman). *History of the Pennsylvania Volunteers, 1861–65*. Vol. 4. Harrisburg, PA: B. Singerly, State Printer, 1869–71, 409.

Congressional Medal of Honor Society. "James Jackson Purman." https://www.cmohs.org/recipients/james-j-purman. Accessed August 13, 2022.

Fraser, Lieutenant Colonel John. "Reports of Lieutenant-Colonel John Fraser, 140th Pennsylvania Infantry, Commanding Regiment and Third Brigade, No. 88." *Official Records*, series 1, vol. 27, part 1. Washington, D.C.: U.S. Government Printing Office, 1880–1901.

Pittsburgh Post-Gazette. "Honorees from Pittsburgh Never Stopped Leading." June 30, 2013, 47.

Wikipedia. "James Jackson Purman." https://en.wikipedia.org/wiki/James_J._Purman. Accessed August 13, 2022.

———. "140th Pennsylvania Infantry Regiment." https://en.wikipedia.org/wiki/140th_Pennsylvania_Infantry_Regiment. Accessed August 13, 2022.

James Milton Pipes

American Civil War. "Medal of Honor." https://americancivilwar.com/medal_of_honor7.html. Accessed August 9, 2022.

Bates, Samuel P. (Samuel Penniman). *History of the Pennsylvania Volunteers, 1861–65*. Vol. 4. Harrisburg, PA: B. Singerly, State Printer, 1869–71, 409.

The Battle of Gettysburg. "140th Pennsylvania Volunteer Infantry Regiment." https://gettysburg.stonesentinels.com/union-monuments/pennsylvania/pennsylvania-infantry/140th-pennsylvania. Accessed August 16, 2022.

Congressional Medal of Honor Society. "James M. Pipes." https://www.cmohs.org/recipients/james-m-pipes. Accessed August 13, 2022.

Fraser, Lieutenant Colonel John. "Reports of Lieutenant-Colonel John Fraser, 140th Pennsylvania Infantry, Commanding Regiment and Third Brigade, No. 88." *Official Records*, series 1, vol. 27, part 1. Washington, D.C.: U.S. Government Printing Office, 1880–1901.

Pittsburgh Post-Gazette. "Honorees from Pittsburgh Never Stopped Leading." June 30, 2013, 47.
Wikipedia. "James Pipes." https://en.wikipedia.org/wiki/James_Pipes. Accessed August 16, 2022.

James Parke Postles

American Civil War. "Medal of Honor." https://americancivilwar.com/medal_of_honor7.html. Accessed August 9, 2022.
Congressional Medal of Honor Society. "James Parke Postles." https://www.cmohs.org/recipients/james-p-postles. Accessed August 9, 2022.
Geni. "Captain James P. Postles, Medal of Honor." https://www.geni.com/people/Capt-James-P-Postles-Medal-of-Honor/6000000016476669147. Accessed August 9, 2022.
Smithsonian National Museum of American History. "Captain James Parke Postles." https://americanhistory.si.edu/collections/search/object/nmah_1411223. Accessed August 9, 2022.
Wikipedia. "James P. Postles." https://en.wikipedia.org/wiki/James_P._Postles. Accessed August 9, 2022.

Daniel Sickles

American Civil War. "Medal of Honor." https://americancivilwar.com/medal_of_honor8.html. Accessed August 10, 2022.
Congressional Medal of Honor Society. "Daniel Edgar Sickles." https://www.cmohs.org/recipients/daniel-e-sickles. Accessed August 10, 2022.
Keneally, Thomas. *American Scoundrel: The Life of the Notorious Civil War General Dan Sickles*. New York: Doubleday, 2002.
Pates, Christopher Ryan. "Daniel Sickles: An Unlikely Union General." HistoryNet. https://www.historynet.com/daniel-sickles-an-unlikely-union-general. Accessed August 10, 2022.
Wikipedia. "Daniel Sickles." https://en.wikipedia.org/wiki/Daniel_Sickles. Accessed August 10, 2022.
———. "Daniel Sickles's Leg." https://en.wikipedia.org/wiki/Daniel_Sickles%27s_leg. Accessed August 10, 2022.

John Lonergan

American Civil War. "Medal of Honor." https://americancivilwar.com/medal_of_honor5.html. Accessed August 10, 2022.

The Battle of Gettysburg. "13th Vermont Volunteer Infantry Regiment." https://gettysburg.stonesentinels.com/union-monuments/vermont/13th-vermont. Accessed August 10, 2022.

Congressional Medal of Honor Society. "John Lonergan." https://www.cmohs.org/recipients/john-lonergan. Accessed August 10, 2022.

Irish American Civil War. "Unveiling of Captain John Lonergan Memorial." https://irishamericancivilwar.com/2010/05/12/unveiling-of-captain-john-lonergan-memorial. Accessed August 10, 2022.

IrishCentral. "On This Day: Tipp Born Captain John Lonergan Was Awarded the Medal of Honor." https://www.irishcentral.com/roots/history/captain-john-lonergan-us-civil-war. Accessed August 10, 2022.

Wikipedia. "13th Vermont Infantry Regiment." https://en.wikipedia.org/wiki/13th_Vermont_Infantry_Regiment. Accessed August 10, 2022.

George Washington Roosevelt

American Civil War. "Medal of Honor." https://americancivilwar.com/medal_of_honor7.html. Accessed August 10, 2022.

Congressional Medal of Honor Society. "George Washington Roosevelt." https://www.cmohs.org/recipients/george-w-roosevelt. Accessed August 10, 2022.

Jones, J.W. *The Story of American Heroism*. Scotts Valley, CA: CreateSpace, 2012.

Military Wiki. "George W. Roosevelt." https://military-history.fandom.com/wiki/George_W._Roosevelt. Accessed August 10, 2022.

———. "26th Pennsylvania Infantry." https://military-history.fandom.com/wiki/26th_Pennsylvania_Infantry. Accessed August 10, 2022.

Wikipedia. "George W. Roosevelt." https://en.wikipedia.org/wiki/George_W._Roosevelt. Accessed August 10, 2022.

Wikiwand. "George W. Roosevelt." https://www.wikiwand.com/en/George_W._Roosevelt. Accessed August 10, 2022.

World War II Forums. "Agents Thwart Sale of Medals of Honor." http://ww2f.com/threads/agents-thwart-sale-of-medals-of-honor.1799. Accessed August 10, 2022.

Part V

Hugh Carey

American Civil War. "Medal of Honor." https://americancivilwar.com/medal_of_honor2.html. Accessed August 9–10, 2022.

Congressional Medal of Honor Society. "Hugh Carey." https://www.cmohs.org/recipients/hugh-carey. Accessed August 10, 2022.

Darrow, Captain John. "Official Reports for the 82nd New York Infantry (Second Militia). Numbers 103." *Official Records*, series 1, vol. 27, part 1. Washington, D.C.: U.S. Government Printing Office, 1880–1901.

New York State Military Museum. "Roster, 82nd Infantry." https://dmna.ny.gov/historic/reghist/civil/rosters/Infantry/82nd_Infantry_CW_Roster.pdf. Accessed August 10, 2022.

Wikipedia. "Hugh Carey (Soldier)." https://en.wikipedia.org/wiki/Hugh_Carey_(soldier). Accessed August 10, 2022.

Frederick Fuger

American Civil War. "Medal of Honor." https://americancivilwar.com/medal_of_honor3.html. Accessed August 11, 2022.

Beyer, W.F., and G.F. Keydel, eds. *Deeds of Valor*. Detroit, MI: Perrien-Keydel Company, 1903.

Congressional Medal of Honor Society. "Frederick Fuger." https://www.cmohs.org/recipients/frederick-w-fuger. Accessed August 11, 2022.

Find A Grave. "Frederick Fuger." https://www.findagrave.com/memorial/5845744/frederick-fuger. Accessed August 11, 2022.

Informational plaque, Battery A, 4th U.S. Artillery, The Angle. Gettysburg National Military Park.

Informational plaque, Battery G, 4th U.S. Artillery. Gettysburg National Cemetery.

Lange, Katie. "U.S. Department of Defense, Medal of Honor Monday: Army 1st Sergeant Frederick Fuger." *DOD News*, June 29, 2020.

Wikipedia. "Frederick W. Fuger." https://en.wikipedia.org/wiki/Frederick_W._F%C3%BCger. Accessed August 11, 2022.

Christopher Flynn

American Civil War. "Medal of Honor." https://americancivilwar.com/medal_of_honor3.html. Accessed August 9, 2022.

Congressional Medal of Honor Society. "Christopher Flynn." https://www.cmohs.org/recipients/christopher-flynn. Accessed August 12, 2022.

Informational Plaque, 14th Connecticut Volunteer Infantry, Hancock Avenue. Gettysburg National Military Park.

Wikipedia. "Christopher Flynn (Medal of Honor)." https://en.wikipedia.org/wiki/Christopher_Flynn_(Medal_of_Honor). Accessed August 12, 2022.

———. "14th Connecticut Infantry Regiment." https://en.wikipedia.org/wiki/14th_Connecticut_Infantry_Regiment. Accessed August 12, 2022.

Elijah William Bacon

American Civil War. "Medal of Honor." https://americancivilwar.com/medal_of_honor1.html. Accessed August 12, 2022.

Congressional Medal of Honor Society. "Elijah William Bacon." https://www.cmohs.org/recipients/elijah-w-bacon. Accessed August 12, 2022.

Informational Plaque, 14th Connecticut Volunteer Infantry, Hancock Avenue. Gettysburg National Military Park.

Wikipedia. "14th Connecticut Infantry Regiment." https://en.wikipedia.org/wiki/14th_Connecticut_Infantry_Regiment. Accessed August 12, 2022.

William B. Hincks

American Civil War. "Medal of Honor." https://americancivilwar.com/medal_of_honor4.html. Accessed August 12, 2022.

Congressional Medal of Honor Society. "William B. Hincks." https://www.cmohs.org/recipients/william-b-hincks. Accessed August 12, 2022.

Informational plaque, 14th Connecticut Volunteer Infantry, Hancock Avenue. Gettysburg National Military Park.

Wikipedia. "14th Connecticut Infantry Regiment." https://en.wikipedia.org/wiki/14th_Connecticut_Infantry_Regiment. Accessed August 12, 2022.

Henry D. O'Brien

American Civil War. "Medal of Honor." https://americancivilwar.com/medal_of_honor7.html. Accessed August 13, 2022.

The Battle of Gettysburg. "1st Minnesota Volunteer Infantry Regiment." https://gettysburg.stonesentinels.com/union-monuments/minnesota/1st-minnesota. Accessed August 13, 2022.

Congressional Medal of Honor Society. "Henry D. O'Brien." https://www.cmohs.org/recipients/henry-d-obrien. Accessed August 13, 2022.

Daily Gopher. "Sacrifice: Remembering the 1st Minnesota at Gettysburg." July 12 2022.

Liberty Rifles. "1st Minnesota Infantry at Gettysburg." https://www.libertyrifles.org/schedule/1st-minnesota. Accessed August 13, 2022.

Minnesota Medal of Honor Memorial. "Henry D. O'Brien Bio." https://www.minnesotamedalofhonormemorial.org/wp-content/uploads/2017/12/OBrien-Henry-Bio-July-16.pdf. Accessed August 13, 2022.

Wikipedia. "1st Minnesota Infantry Regiment." https://en.wikipedia.org/wiki/1st_Minnesota_Infantry_Regiment. Accessed August 13, 2022.

———. "Henry D. O'Brien." https://en.wikipedia.org/wiki/Henry_D._O%27Brien. Accessed August 13, 2022.

John H. Robinson

American Civil War. "Medal of Honor." https://americancivilwar.com/medal_of_honor7.html. Accessed August 13, 2022.

Congressional Medal of Honor Society. "John H. Robinson." https://www.cmohs.org/recipients/john-h-robinson. Accessed August 13, 2022.

Devereux, Colonel Arthur. "Official Report of Col. Arthur F. Devereux, 19th Massachusetts Infantry, No. 110." *Official Records*, series 1, vol. 27, part 1. Washington, D.C.: U.S. Government Printing Office, 1880–1901.

Historical Digression. "19th Massachusetts Infantry at Gettysburg." https://historicaldigression.com/2014/07/03/19th-massachusetts-infantry-at-gettysburg. Accessed August 13, 2022.

Waitt, Ernest Linden. *History of the Nineteenth Regiment, Massachusetts Volunteer Infantry*. Reprint ed. Baltimore, MD: Butternut and Blue, 1998.

Wikipedia. "John H. Robinson (Medal of Honor)." https://en.wikipedia.org/wiki/John_H._Robinson_(Medal_of_Honor). Accessed August 13, 2022.

Joseph H. DeCastro

American Battlefield Trust. "Joseph H. DeCastro: The First Hispanic Recipient of the Medal of Honor." https://www.battlefields.org/learn/biographies/joseph-h-de-castro. Accessed August 13, 2022.

American Civil War. "Medal of Honor." https://americancivilwar.com/medal_of_honor2.html. Accessed August 13, 2022.

Congressional Medal of Honor Society. "Joseph H. DeCastro." https://www.cmohs.org/recipients/joseph-h-decastro. Accessed August 13, 2022.

Devereux, Colonel Arthur. "Official Report of Col. Arthur F. Devereux, 19th Massachusetts Infantry, No. 110." *Official Records*, series 1, vol. 27, part 1. Washington, D.C.: U.S. Government Printing Office, 1880–1901.

Historical Digression. "19th Massachusetts Infantry at Gettysburg." https://historicaldigression.com/2014/07/03/19th-massachusetts-infantry-at-gettysburg. Accessed August 13, 2022.

Waitt, Ernest Linden. *History of the Nineteenth Regiment, Massachusetts Volunteer Infantry*. Reprint ed. Baltimore, MD: Butternut and Blue, 1998.

Benjamin H. Jellison

American Civil War. "Medal of Honor." https://americancivilwar.com/medal_of_honor5.html. Accessed August 13, 2022.

Brooklyn Daily Eagle. "Gettysburg Hero Dies." April 6, 1924, 41.

Congressional Medal of Honor Society. "Benjamin H. Jellison." https://www.cmohs.org/recipients/benjamin-h-jellison. Accessed August 13, 2022.

Devereux, Colonel Arthur. "Official Report of Col. Arthur F. Devereux, 19th Massachusetts Infantry, No. 110." *Official Records*, series 1, vol. 27, part 1. Washington, D.C.: U.S. Government Printing Office, 1880–1901.

Historical Digression. "19th Massachusetts Infantry at Gettysburg." https://historicaldigression.com/2014/07/03/19th-massachusetts-infantry-at-gettysburg. Accessed August 13, 2022.

Waitt, Ernest Linden. *History of the Nineteenth Regiment, Massachusetts Volunteer Infantry*. Reprint ed. Baltimore, MD: Butternut and Blue, 1998.

Benjamin Franklin Falls

Adams, Captain John G.B. *Reminiscences of the Nineteenth Massachusetts Regiment*. Boston: Wright, Potter Printing Company, 1899.

American Civil War. "Medal of Honor." https://americancivilwar.com/medal_of_honor3.html. Accessed August 13, 2022.

Congressional Medal of Honor Society. "Benjamin Franklin Falls." https://www.cmohs.org/recipients/benjamin-f-falls. Accessed August 13, 2022.

Devereux, Colonel Arthur. "Official Report of Col. Arthur F. Devereux, 19th Massachusetts Infantry, No. 110." *Official Records*, series 1, vol. 27, part 1. Washington, D.C.: U.S. Government Printing Office, 1880–1901.

Find A Grave. "Benjamin Franklin Falls." https://www.findagrave.com/memorial/21140/benjamin-franklin-falls. Accessed August 13, 2022.

Historical Digression. "19th Massachusetts Infantry at Gettysburg." https://historicaldigression.com/2014/07/03/19th-massachusetts-infantry-at-gettysburg. Accessed August 13, 2022.

Waitt, Ernest Linden. *History of the Nineteenth Regiment, Massachusetts Volunteer Infantry*. Reprint ed. Baltimore, MD: Butternut and Blue, 1998.

Wikipedia. "Benjamin Franklin Falls." https://en.wikipedia.org/wiki/Benjamin_Franklin_Falls. Accessed August 13, 2022.

William E. Miller

American Battlefield Trust. "Gettysburg—East Cavalry Field, July 3, 1863." https://www.battlefields.org/learn/maps/gettysburg-east-cavalry-field-july-3-1863. Accessed August 14, 2022.

American Civil War. "Medal of Honor." https://americancivilwar.com/medal_of_honor6.html. Accessed August 14, 2022.

Congressional Medal of Honor Society. "William E. Miller." https://www.cmohs.org/recipients/william-e-miller. Accessed August 14, 2022.

Find A Grave. "William Edward Miller." https://www.findagrave.com/memorial/5831588/william-edward-miller. Accessed August 14, 2022.

Holbrook, Thomas. "Men of Action: The Unsung Heroes of East Cavalry Field, Unsung Heroes of Gettysburg." Gettysburg Seminar Papers, National Park Service. http://npshistory.com/series/symposia/gettysburg_seminars/5/essay5.htm. Accessed August 14, 2022.

Task and Purpose. "How a Civil War Soldier Who Disobeyed Orders Earned the Medal of Honor at Gettysburg." https://taskandpurpose.com/news/civil-war-medal-of-honor-gettysburg. Accessed August 14, 2022.

Wikipedia. "3rd Pennsylvania Cavalry." https://en.wikipedia.org/wiki/3rd_Pennsylvania_Cavalry. Accessed August 14, 2022.

John B. Mayberry

American Civil War. "Medal of Honor." https://americancivilwar.com/medal_of_honor6.html. Accessed August 15, 2022.

Antietam on the Web. "Medal of Honor Citation—Private John B. Mayberry." https://antietam.aotw.org/moh.php?citation_id=125. Accessed August 15, 2022.

The Battle of Gettysburg. "1st Delaware Volunteer Infantry Regiment." https://gettysburg.stonesentinels.com/union-monuments/delaware/1st-delaware. Accessed August 15, 2022.

Congressional Medal of Honor Society. "John B. Mayberry." https://www.cmohs.org/recipients/john-b-mayberry. Accessed August 15, 2022.

Find A Grave. "John B. Maberry." https://www.findagrave.com/memorial/7122546/john-b-maberry. Accessed August 15, 2022.

Bernard McCarren

American Civil War. "Medal of Honor." https://americancivilwar.com/medal_of_honor6.html. Accessed August 15, 2022.

Antietam on the Web. "Federal (USV) Corporal Bernard McCarren." https://antietam.aotw.org/officers.php?officer_id=1008. Accessed August 15, 2022.

The Battle of Gettysburg. "1st Delaware Volunteer Infantry Regiment." https://gettysburg.stonesentinels.com/union-monuments/delaware/1st-delaware. Accessed August 15, 2022.

Congressional Medal of Honor Society. "Bernard McCarren." https://www.cmohs.org/recipients/bernard-mccarren. Accessed August 15, 2022.

Pickett, Russ. "Bernard McCarren, One of Delaware's Medal of Honor Recipients." http://www.russpickett.com/history/mccarren.htm. Accessed August 15, 2022.

Wikipedia. "Bernard McCarren." https://en.wikipedia.org/wiki/Bernard_McCarren. Accessed August 15, 2022.

William H. Raymond

American Civil War. “Medal of Honor.” https://americancivilwar.com/medal_of_honor7.html. Accessed August 15, 2022.

The Battle of Gettysburg. “108th New York Volunteer Infantry Regiment.” https://gettysburg.stonesentinels.com/union-monuments/new-york/new-york-infantry/108th-new-york. Accessed August 15, 2022.

Congressional Medal of Honor Society. “William H. Raymond.” https://www.cmohs.org/recipients/william-h-raymond. Accessed August 15, 2022.

Find A Grave. “William H. Raymond.” https://www.findagrave.com/memorial/18820/william-h-raymond. Accessed August 15, 2022.

Marcotte, Bob. “The Civil War Battles of Lt. Col. Francis Edwin Pierce, 108th New York Volunteer Infantry.” *Rochester History* 65, no. 2 (Spring 2003): 11–13.

Rochester Democrat and Chronicle. “Medal of Honor—Recognition of Gallant Conduct of Lieutenant Raymond.” March 11, 1896, 15.

Washburn, Private George H. *A Complete Military History and Record of the 108th Regiment N.Y. Vols. from 1862 to 1894*. Rochester, NY, 1894.

Wikipedia. “William H. Raymond.” https://en.wikipedia.org/wiki/William_H._Raymond. Accessed August 15, 2022.

Alexander Stewart Webb

American Civil War. “Medal of Honor.” https://americancivilwar.com/medal_of_honor8.html. Accessed August 16, 2022.

The Battle of Gettysburg. “Alexander Webb.” https://gettysburg.stonesentinels.com/monuments-to-individuals/alexander-webb. Accessed August 16, 2022.

Congressional Medal of Honor Society. “Alexander S. Webb.” https://www.cmohs.org/recipients/alexander-s-webb. Accessed August 16, 2022.

United States Senate, 54th Congress, 1st Session, Report No. 58. “Bvt. Maj. Gen. Alexander Stewart Webb.” Washington, D.C., February 4, 1896.

Wikipedia. “Alexander Webb.” https://en.wikipedia.org/wiki/Alexander_S._Webb. Accessed August 16, 2022.

James Wiley

American Civil War. "Medal of Honor." https://americancivilwar.com/medal_of_honor8.html. Accessed August 16, 2022.

The Battle of Gettysburg. "59th New York Volunteer Infantry Regiment." https://gettysburg.stonesentinels.com/union-monuments/new-york/new-york-infantry/59th-new-york. Accessed August 16, 2022.

The Civil War in the East. "59th New York Volunteer Infantry Regiment." https://civilwarintheeast.com/us-regiments-batteries/new-york-infantry/59th-new-york. Accessed August 16, 2022.

Congressional Medal of Honor Society. "James Wiley." https://www.cmohs.org/recipients/james-wiley. Accessed August 16, 2022.

Veteran Tributes. "James B. Wiley." http://veterantributes.org/TributeDetail.php?recordID=1687. Accessed August 16, 2022.

Wikipedia. "59th New York Infantry Regiment." https://en.wikipedia.org/wiki/59th_New_York_Infantry_Regiment. Accessed August 16, 2022.

———. "James Wiley (Medal of Honor)." https://en.wikipedia.org/wiki/James_Wiley_(Medal_of_Honor). Accessed August 16, 2022.

George H. Dore

American Civil War. "Medal of Honor." https://americancivilwar.com/medal_of_honor2.html. Accessed August 9, 2022.

The Battle of Gettysburg. "126th New York Volunteer Infantry Regiment." https://gettysburg.stonesentinels.com/union-monuments/new-york/new-york-infantry/126th-new-york. Accessed August 16, 2022.

The Comprehensive Guide to the Victoria and George Cross. "George Henry Dore." http://www.vconline.org.uk/george-h-dore/4591843577.html. Accessed August 16, 2022.

Congressional Medal of Honor Society. "George H. Dore." https://www.cmohs.org/recipients/george-h-dore. Accessed August 16, 2022.

Dan Masters' Civil War Chronicles. "Stopping Pickett's Charge: The 126th New York at Gettysburg." https://dan-masters-civil-war.blogspot.com/2020/02/stopping-picketts-charge-126th-new-york.html. Accessed August 16, 2022.

New York State Military Museum and Veterans Research Center. "126th Infantry Regiment." https://museum.dmna.ny.gov/unit-history/infantry-2/126th-infantry-regiment. Accessed August 16, 2022.

WikiFox. "George H. Dore." https://www.wikifox.org/en/wiki/George_H._Dore. Accessed August 16, 2022.

Jerry Wall

American Civil War. "Medal of Honor." https://americancivilwar.com/medal_of_honor8.html. Accessed August 9, 2022.

The Battle of Gettysburg. "126th New York Volunteer Infantry Regiment." https://gettysburg.stonesentinels.com/union-monuments/new-york/new-york-infantry/126th-new-york. Accessed August 16, 2022.

Beagle, Ben. "Hero of Pickett's Charge with New Plaque: Dansville Remembers Medal of Honor Recipient." *Livingston County News*, November 14, 2018.

Congressional Medal of Honor Society. "Jerry C. Wall." https://www.cmohs.org/recipients/jerry-c-wall. Accessed August 16, 2022.

Dan Masters' Civil War Chronicles. "Stopping Pickett's Charge: The 126th New York at Gettysburg." https://dan-masters-civil-war.blogspot.com/2020/02/stopping-picketts-charge-126th-new-york.html. Accessed August 16, 2022.

New York State Military Museum and Veterans Research Center. "126th Infantry Regiment." https://museum.dmna.ny.gov/unit-history/infantry-2/126th-infantry-regiment. Accessed August 16, 2022.

Morris Brown Jr.

American Civil War. "Medal of Honor." https://americancivilwar.com/medal_of_honor1.html. Accessed August 16, 2022.

The Battle of Gettysburg. "126th New York Volunteer Infantry Regiment." https://gettysburg.stonesentinels.com/union-monuments/new-york/new-york-infantry/126th-new-york. Accessed August 16, 2022.

Congressional Medal of Honor Society. "Morris Brown, Jr." https://www.cmohs.org/recipients/morris-brown-jr. Accessed August 16, 2022.

Dan Masters' Civil War Chronicles. "Stopping Pickett's Charge: The 126th New York at Gettysburg." https://dan-masters-civil-war.blogspot.com/2020/02/stopping-picketts-charge-126th-new-york.html. Accessed August 16, 2022.

New York State Military Museum and Veterans Research Center. "126th Infantry Regiment." https://museum.dmna.ny.gov/unit-history/infantry-2/126th-infantry-regiment. Accessed August 16, 2022.

Wheelock Graves Veazey

American Civil War. "Medal of Honor." https://americancivilwar.com/medal_of_honor8.html. Accessed August 17, 2022.

Beyer, W.F., and G.F. Keydel, eds. *Deeds of Valor*. Detroit, MI: Perrien-Keydel Company, 1903.

Congressional Medal of Honor Society. "Wheelock G. Veazey." https://www.cmohs.org/recipients/wheelock-g-veazey. Accessed August 17, 2022.

New England Historical Society. "Wheelock Veazey Tries to Stay Awake at the Battle of Gettysburg." https://www.newenglandhistoricalsociety.com/wheelock-veazey-tries-to-stay-awake-at-the-battle-of-gettysburg. Accessed August 17, 2022.

Ullery, Jacob. *Men of Vermont: An Illustrated Biographical History of Vermonters and Sons of Vermont*. Brattleboro, VT: Transcript Publishing Company, 1894.

Wikipedia. "Wheelock G. Veazey." https://en.wikipedia.org/wiki/Wheelock_G._Veazey. Accessed August 17, 2022.

Marshall Sherman

American Civil War. "Medal of Honor." https://americancivilwar.com/medal_of_honor8.html. Accessed August 17, 2022.

Congressional Medal of Honor Society. "Marshall Sherman." https://www.cmohs.org/recipients/marshall-sherman. Accessed August 17, 2022.

Loyal Legion of the United States. *Glimpses of the Nation's Struggle: Papers Read Before the Minnesota Commandery of the Military Order of the Loyal Legion of the United States, 1892–1897*. Vol. 3. Minneapolis: Minnesota MOLLUS, 1897.

Minnesota Historical Society. "Marshall Sherman." https://www.mnhs.org/education/resources/marshall-sherman. Accessed August 17, 2022.

Wikipedia. "Marshall Sherman." https://en.wikipedia.org/wiki/Marshall_Sherman. Accessed August 17, 2022.

William Wells

American Civil War. "Medal of Honor." https://americancivilwar.com/medal_of_honor2.html. Accessed August 17, 2022.

The Battle of Gettysburg. "William Wells." https://gettysburg.stonesentinels.com/monuments-to-individuals/william-wells. Accessed August 17, 2022.

Congressional Medal of Honor Society. "William Wells." https://www.cmohs.org/recipients/william-wells-1. Accessed August 17, 2022.

Find A Grave. "William Wells." https://www.findagrave.com/memorial/22669/william-wells. Accessed August 17, 2022.

Wikipedia. "William Wells (General)." https://en.wikipedia.org/wiki/William_Wells_(general). Accessed August 17, 2022.

John E. Clopp

American Civil War. "Medal of Honor." https://americancivilwar.com/medal_of_honor2.html. Accessed August 17, 2022.

Bates, Samuel P. (Samuel Penniman). *History of the Pennsylvania Volunteers, 1861–65*. Vol. 2. Harrisburg, PA: B. Singerly, State Printer, 1869–71, 797–99.

Congressional Medal of Honor Society. "John Clopp." https://www.cmohs.org/recipients/john-e-clopp. Accessed August 17, 2022.

Lash, Gary George. *Duty Well Done: The History of Edward Baker's California Regiment (71st Pennsylvania)*. Army of the Potomac Series. Baltimore, MD: Butternut & Blue, 2001.

Smith, Colonel R. Penn. "Report of Col. R. Penn Smith, 71st Pennsylvania Infantry, No. 106." *Official Records*, series 1, vol. 27, part 1. Washington, D.C.: U.S. Government Printing Office, 1880–1901.

Wikipedia. "John E. Clopp." https://en.wikipedia.org/wiki/John_E._Clopp. Accessed August 17, 2022

———. "71st Pennsylvania Infantry Regiment." https://en.wikipedia.org/wiki/71st_Pennsylvania_Infantry_Regiment. Accessed August 17, 2022.

George Greenville (Grenville) Benedict

American Civil War. "Medal of Honor." https://americancivilwar.com/medal_of_honor1.html. Accessed August 19, 2022.

The Battle of Gettysburg. "State of Vermont." https://gettysburg.stonesentinels.com/union-monuments/vermont/state-of-vermont. Accessed August 19, 2022.

Congressional Medal of Honor Society. "George G. Benedict." https://www.cmohs.org/recipients/george-g-benedict. Accessed August 19, 2022.

Goodrich, J.E. "Colonel George G. Benedict, A.M., L.H.D." *Proceedings of the New York State Historical Association*. Vol. 8. Ithaca, NY: Cornell University Press, 1909.

Iron Brigader. "General George Stannard and the 2nd Vermont at Gettysburg." https://ironbrigader.com/2016/07/31/general-george-stannard-2nd-vermont-brigade-gettysburg. Accessed August 19, 2022.

Wikipedia. "George Grenville Benedict." https://en.wikipedia.org/wiki/George_Grenville_Benedict. Accessed August 19, 2022.

———. "12th Vermont Infantry Regiment." https://en.wikipedia.org/wiki/12th_Vermont_Infantry_Regiment. Accessed August 19, 2022.

Oliver P. Rood

American Civil War. "Medal of Honor." https://americancivilwar.com/medal_of_honor7.html. Accessed August 19, 2022.

The Battle of Gettysburg. "14th Indiana Volunteer Infantry Regiment." https://gettysburg.stonesentinels.com/union-monuments/indiana/14th-indiana. Accessed August 19, 2022.

———. "Hoke's Brigade." https://gettysburg.stonesentinels.com/confederate-headquarters/hokes-brigade. Accessed August 19, 2022.

Congressional Medal of Honor Society. "Oliver P Rood." https://www.cmohs.org/recipients/oliver-p-rood. Accessed August 19, 2022.

Rood, Oliver. "Vote as You Shot." Brownstown *(IN) Banner*, August 12, 1880, 1.

Vigo County Historical Society. "Roster of the 14th Indiana Infantry, Company F." https://ranger95.com/civil_war_us/indiana/infantry/14in_inf/14in_inf_rgt_rost_f.htm. Accessed August 19, 2022.

Wikipedia. "Oliver P. Rood." https://en.wikipedia.org/wiki/Oliver_P._Rood. Accessed August 19, 2022.

———. "20th Indiana Infantry Regiment." https://en.wikipedia.org/wiki/20th_Indiana_Infantry_Regiment. Accessed August 19, 2022.

John G. Miller

American Civil War. "Medal of Honor." https://americancivilwar.com/medal_of_honor6.html. Accessed August 19, 2022.

The Battle of Gettysburg. "8th Ohio Volunteer Infantry Regiment." https://gettysburg.stonesentinels.com/union-monuments/ohio/8th-ohio. Accessed August 19, 2022.

Congressional Medal of Honor Society. "John G. Miller." https://www.cmohs.org/recipients/john-g-miller. Accessed August 19, 2022.

Hartzell, Stephen J., comp. "Roster of the 8th Regt., Ohio Volunteer Infantry." http://www.historynotebook.com/8thOVI.html#Co-G. Accessed August 19, 2022.

Wikipedia. "John G. Miller, (Medal of Honor)." https://en.wikipedia.org/wiki/John_G._Miller_(Medal_of_Honor). Accessed August 19, 2022.

WikiTree. "38th Regiment, Virginia Infantry (Pittsylvania Regiment), United States Civil War." https://www.wikitree.com/wiki/Space:38th_Regiment%2C_Virginia_Infantry_(Pittsylvania_Regiment)%2C_United_States_Civil_War. Accessed August 19, 2022.

James Richmond

American Civil War. "Medal of Honor." https://americancivilwar.com/medal_of_honor7.html. Accessed August 21, 2022.

The Battle of Gettysburg. "8th Ohio Volunteer Infantry Regiment." https://gettysburg.stonesentinels.com/union-monuments/ohio/8th-ohio. Accessed August 21, 2022.

Congressional Medal of Honor Society. "James Richmond." https://www.cmohs.org/recipients/james-richmond. Accessed August 21, 2022.

Hartzell, Stephen J., comp. "Roster of the 8th Regt., Ohio Volunteer Infantry." http://www.historynotebook.com/8thOVI.html#Co-G. Accessed August 19, 2022.

Wikipedia. "John G. Miller (Medal of Honor)." https://en.wikipedia.org/wiki/John_G._Miller_(Medal_of_Honor). Accessed August 21, 2022.

WikiTree. "38th Regiment, Virginia Infantry (Pittsylvania Regiment), United States Civil War." https://www.wikitree.com/wiki/Space:38th_Regiment%2C_Virginia_Infantry_(Pittsylvania_Regiment)%2C_United_States_Civil_War. Accessed August 19, 2022.

Edmund Rice

Adams, Captain John G.B. *Reminiscences of the Nineteenth Massachusetts Regiment.* Boston: Wright, Potter Printing Company, 1899.

American Civil War. "Medal of Honor." https://americancivilwar.com/medal_of_honor7.html. Accessed August 21, 2022.

Arlington National Cemetery. "Edmund Rice—Brigadier General, United States Army." https://www.arlingtoncemetery.net/edmundri.htm. Accessed August 21, 2022.

Congressional Medal of Honor Society. "Edmund Rice." https://www.cmohs.org/recipients/edmund-rice. Accessed August 21, 2022.

Devereux, Colonel Arthur. "Official Report of Col. Arthur F. Devereux, 19th Massachusetts Infantry, No. 110." *Official Records*, series 1, vol. 27, part 1. Washington, D.C.: U.S. Government Printing Office, 1880–1901.

Wikipedia. "Edmund Rice (Medal of Honor)." https://en.wikipedia.org/wiki/Edmund_Rice_(Medal_of_Honor). Accessed August 21, 2022.

Alonzo Cushing

American Civil War. "Medal of Honor." https://americancivilwar.com/medal_of_honor2.html. Accessed August 21, 2022.

Congressional Medal of Honor Society. "Alonzo H. Cushing." https://www.cmohs.org/recipients/alonzo-h-cushing. Accessed August 21, 2022.

Find A Grave. "Alonzo Hereford Cushing." https://www.findagrave.com/memorial/3657/alonzo-hereford-cushing. Accessed August 21, 2022.

National Park Service. "Lt. Alonzo Cushing at Gettysburg." https://www.nps.gov/gett/learn/historyculture/cushing-at-gettysburg.htm. Accessed August 21, 2022.

U.S. Army. "First Lieutenant Alonzo H. Cushing, Medal of Honor." https://www.army.mil/medalofhonor/cushing.

White House. "President Obama Awards the Medal of Honor to First Lieutenant Alonzo H. Cushing." November 6, 2014. https://obamawhitehouse.archives.gov/blog/2014/11/06/president-obama-awards-medal-honor-first-lieutenant-alonzo-h-cushing. Accessed August 21, 2022.

Wikipedia. "Alonzo Cushing." https://en.wikipedia.org/wiki/Alonzo_Cushing. Accessed August 21, 2022.

James B. Thompson

American Civil War. "Medal of Honor." https://americancivilwar.com/medal_of_honor8.html. Accessed August 22, 2022.

Bates, Samuel P. (Samuel Penniman). *History of the Pennsylvania Volunteers, 1861–65*. Vol. 1. Harrisburg, PA: B. Singerly, State Printer, 1869–71, 919–20.

Congressional Medal of Honor Society. "James B. Thompson." https://www.cmohs.org/recipients/james-b-thompson. Accessed August 22, 2022.

Find A Grave. "James B. Thompson." https://www.findagrave.com/memorial/7224349/james-b.-thompson. Accessed August 22, 2022.

Gettysburg National Military Park. "From the Fields of Gettysburg: A Correction on Colonel DuBose and His 15th Georgia Infantry on July 3." https://npsgnmp.wordpress.com/2016/07/22/a-correction-on-colonel-dubose-and-his-15th-georgia-infantry-on-july-3. Accessed August 22, 2022.

Pennsylvania Volunteers of the Civil War. "42nd Pennsylvania Regiment." http://www.pacivilwar.com/regiment/42nd.html. Accessed August 22, 2022.

Roster of the 42nd Pennsylvania Regiment. https://www.pa-roots.com/pacw/reserves/13thres/13threscog.html. Accessed August 22, 2022.

Roster of the 190th Regiment Pennsylvania Volunteers. https://www.pa-roots.com/pacw/infantry/190th/190thcof.html. Accessed August 22, 2022.

Wikipedia. "James B. Thompson." https://en.wikipedia.org/wiki/James_B._Thompson. Accessed August 22, 2022.

Harvey May Munsell

American Civil War. "Medal of Honor." https://americancivilwar.com/medal_of_honor6.html. Accessed August 23, 2022.

The Battle of Gettysburg. "99th Pennsylvania Volunteer Infantry Regiment." https://gettysburg.stonesentinels.com/union-monuments/pennsylvania/pennsylvania-infantry/99th-pennsylvania. Accessed August 23, 2022.

Beyer, W.F., and G.F. Keydel, eds. *Deeds of Valor*. Detroit, MI: Perrien-Keydel Company, 1903.

Civil War in the East. "99th Pennsylvania Volunteer Infantry Regiment." https://civilwarintheeast.com/us-regiments-batteries/pennsylvania/99th-pennsylvania-infantry. Accessed August 23, 2022.

Congressional Medal of Honor Society. "Harvey M. Munsell." https://www.cmohs.org/recipients/harvey-m-munsell. Accessed August 23, 2022.

HistoryNet. "Fighting and Dying for the Colors at Gettysburg." https://www.historynet.com/fighting-and-dying-for-the-colors-at-gettysburg/?f. Accessed August 23, 2022.

Wikipedia. "Harvey M. Munsell." https://en.wikipedia.org/wiki/Harvey_M._Munsell. Accessed August 23, 2022.

George Crawford Platt

American Battlefield Trust. "Battle of Fairfield." https://www.battlefields.org/learn/articles/battle-fairfield. Accessed August 23, 2022.

American Civil War. "Medal of Honor." https://americancivilwar.com/medal_of_honor7.html. Accessed August 23, 2022.

The Battle of Gettysburg. "6th United States Cavalry Regiment." https://gettysburg.stonesentinels.com/us-regulars/us-cavalry/6th-us-cavalry. Accessed August 23, 2022.

Civil War Album. "Battle of Fairfield, PA." http://www.civilwaralbum.com/misc5/fairfield1.htm. Accessed August 23, 2022.

Civil War in the East. "6th United States Cavalry." https://civilwarintheeast.com/us-regiments-batteries/us-regulars/6th-united-states-cavalry. Accessed August 23, 2022.

Congressional Medal of Honor Society. "George C. Platt." https://www.cmohs.org/recipients/george-c-platt. Accessed August 23, 2022.

Find A Grave. "George Crawford." https://www.findagrave.com/memorial/7205659/george-crawford-platt. Accessed August 23, 2022.

Thomas, Sarah Sites, Tim Smith, Gary Kross and Dean S. Thomas. *Fairfield in the Civil War*. Gettysburg, PA: Thomas Publications, 2011.

Wikipedia. "George Crawford Platt." https://en.wikipedia.org/wiki/George_Crawford_Platt. Accessed August 23, 2022.

Martin Schwenk

American Battlefield Trust. "Battle of Fairfield." https://www.battlefields.org/learn/articles/battle-fairfield. Accessed August 23, 2022.

American Civil War. "Medal of Honor." https://americancivilwar.com/medal_of_honor8.html. Accessed August 23, 2022.

The Battle of Gettysburg. "6th United States Cavalry Regiment." https://gettysburg.stonesentinels.com/us-regulars/us-cavalry/6th-us-cavalry. Accessed August 23, 2022.
Civil War Album. "Battle of Fairfield, PA." http://www.civilwaralbum.com/misc5/fairfield1.htm. Accessed August 23, 2022.
Civil War in the East. "6th United States Cavalry." https://civilwarintheeast.com/us-regiments-batteries/us-regulars/6th-united-states-cavalry. Accessed August 23, 2022.
Congressional Medal of Honor Society. "Martin Schwenk." https://www.cmohs.org/recipients/martin-schwenk. Accessed August 23, 2022.
Thomas, Sarah Sites, Tim Smith, Gary Kross and Dean S. Thomas. *Fairfield in the Civil War*. Gettysburg, PA: Thomas Publications, 2011.
Wikipedia. "Martin Schwenk." https://en.wikipedia.org/wiki/Martin_Schwenk. Accessed August 23, 2022.

Part VI

Charles Capehart

American Civil War. "Medal of Honor." https://americancivilwar.com/medal_of_honor2.html. Accessed June 12, 2022.
Capehart, Major Charles E. "Report of Major Charles E. Capehart, First West Virginia Cavalry." *Official Records*, serial 043, series I, vol. 27, chapter 39. Washington, D.C.: U.S. Government Printing Office, 1880–1901.
Congressional Medal of Honor Society. "Charles E. Capehart." https://www.cmohs.org/recipients/charles-e-capehart, Accessed June 12, 2022.
Monterey Pass Battlefield Park and Museum. "The Story of the Battle." https://montereypassbattlefield.org/about. Accessed June 12, 2022.

Charles Maynard (Myron) Holton

American Battlefield Trust. "Falling Waters—July 14, 1863." https://www.battlefields.org/learn/maps/falling-waters-july-14-1863. Accessed August 24, 2022.
American Civil War. "Medal of Honor." https://americancivilwar.com/medal_of_honor4.html. Accessed August 9, 2022.

Beyer, W.F., and G.F. Keydel, eds. *Deeds of Valor*. Detroit, MI: Perrien-Keydel Company, 1903.

The Civil War in the East. "55th Virginia Infantry Regiment." https://civilwarintheeast.com/confederate-regiments/virginia/55th-virginia-infantry-regiment. Accessed August 24, 2022.

Congressional Medal of Honor Society. "Charles M. Holton." https://www.cmohs.org/recipients/charles-m-holton. Accessed August 24, 2022.

Find A Grave. "Charles Maynard Holton." https://www.findagrave.com/memorial/6922828/charles-maynard-holton. Accessed August 24, 2022.

Wikipedia. "Charles M. Holton." https://en.wikipedia.org/wiki/Charles_M._Holton. Accessed August 24, 2022.

———. "Michigan Brigade." https://en-academic.com/dic.nsf/enwiki/294478#Organization_and_the_Gettysburg_Campaign. Accessed August 24, 2022.

Appendix A

HistoryNet. "Fighting and Dying for the Colors at Gettysburg." https://www.historynet.com/fighting-and-dying-for-the-colors-at-gettysburg/?f. Accessed August 23, 2022.

Appendix B

Congressional Medal of Honor Society. "The Medal of Honor." https://www.cmohs.org/medal. Accessed August 23, 2022.

INDEX

C

D

E

F

G

R

S

T

U

V

W

Z

ABOUT THE AUTHOR

Jim Gindlesperger is a retired safety manager from Carnegie Mellon University, where he served as a consultant on a project between Google, NASA, *National Geographic* and Carnegie Mellon to map and photograph Civil War sites using high-resolution robotic cameras with 360-degree capability. He has coauthored three books with his wife, Suzanne, and five additional books on his own. Jim has contributed articles to *Gettysburg Magazine* and *Johnstown Magazine* and writes a monthly article on Civil War Medal of Honor recipients for the Congressional Medal of Honor Society's daily blog. He sits on the advisory committee for the National Museum of Civil War Medicine, and his book *Bullets and Bandages* won the Bachelder-Coddington Literary Award as the best book on the Gettysburg Campaign for 2020.